Music and Language

Music and Language

The Rise of Western Music
as Exemplified in Settings of the Mass

THRASYBULOS GEORGIADES

translated by
Marie Louise Göllner
Professor of Music,
University of California, Los Angeles

Cambridge University Press
Cambridge
London   New York   New Rochelle
Sydney   Melbourne

Published by the Press Syndicate of the University of Cambridge
The Pitt Building, Trumpington Street, Cambridge CB2 1RP
32 East 57th Street, New York, NY 10022, USA
296 Beaconsfield Parade, Middle Park, Melbourne 3206, Australia

Originally published in German as *Musik und Sprache*, 2nd edition, by
Springer-Verlag, Heidelberg, 1974 and © Springer-Verlag, 1974.

Now first published in English by Cambridge University Press 1982 as
Music and Language.
© Cambridge University Press 1982

Printed in Great Britain at the University Press, Cambridge

Library of Congress catalogue card number: 82–4246

British Library Cataloguing in Publication Data
Georgiades, Thrasybulos
Music and language.
1. Mass (Music)
I. Title   II. Musik und Sprache. *English*
783.2'1   ML3088

ISBN 0 521 23309 7 hard covers
ISBN 0 521 29902 0 paperback

WD

Contents

Preface

The present book is based on a lecture-course dealing with the musical setting of the Mass which was held at the University of Heidelberg during the summer semester of 1952, and on a series of lectures delivered for South German radio (January to March 1953) on the same subject. The tone of oral communication resulting from this origin has been retained.

Even in the original context it was not my purpose to present the musical category of the Mass as a separate historical phenomenon but rather to shed light on European music as a whole from a particular angle. For this reason I have also included some material from my lecture-course (winter semester 1948–9) on the formation and growth of Western music.

This brief work is thus not intended as a speculative treatment on the theme of music and language nor as a history of the musical setting of the Mass, nor yet as the presentation of each individual phase of European music in the manner of a condensed textbook on music history.

The reader not familiar with the subject matter is therefore urged to consult one of the many brief histories of music on the market. It is, however, vitally important that the reader attempt in each case to familiarize himself with the music under consideration, a task for which the few musical examples included in the book can provide only an incentive. From chapter 10 (that is, from Bach) onward, examples have been omitted almost entirely, since the works referred to are readily accessible in modern editions.

For the help which Dr. Irmgard Hermann-Bengen has given me from the preparation of the manuscript to the completion of its printing I should like to express my deep appreciation.

Heidelberg, 28 March 1954   TG

Translator's Foreword

What are the forces behind Western music which have been responsible for the unique course of its history? And can this history be
viewed as an organic whole rather than as an unrelated series of
events? As a native of Athens who completed his education in
Germany, Thrasybulos Georgiades (1907–77) was struck by the
fundamental differences in the underlying concept of rhythm
between the ancient classical languages, Greek and Latin, on the one
hand and those of the Western world, in particular German, on the
other. In exploring the effect which these differences have had on
music as the rhythmic setting of language he arrived at an essentially
new approach to an interpretation of its history, one in which music
is placed in the center of man's creative–intellectual endeavors and
is thus dependent not only on technical changes within its own
boundaries but also on changing concepts of religion and philosophy.

In the present book, written shortly after he became Professor of
Musicology at the University of Heidelberg, Georgiades expresses the
basic tenets of this new approach, laying the foundation on which he
was to build for the remainder of his life. To point out as clearly as
possible the changes which have taken place within Western music he
here focuses on the one text which has remained constant throughout its history, that of the Mass. And in following this path he singles
out particularly the ninth century as the beginning of polyphony;
the Reformation and its effects on music, culminating in the works
of Heinrich Schütz; and the Viennese classical composers, Haydn,
Mozart and Beethoven.

One of Georgiades' main concerns in applying his distinctive
method to the discipline was the choice of a terminology adequate
to the expression of new ideas, in particular one whose meaning
could be determined with precision. He thus sought to clarify and
limit the use of many words which had become diffuse and vacillat-
ory in their meaning during the nineteenth century. The translation
endeavors to reflect this concern by avoiding such overworked words
as "style" and "evolution" and by confining others to a specific
technical sense, as in the distinction between "tone" as the sounding
and "note" as the written element of music.

The necessary counterpart of the basic view of music and its history here expressed is to be found in a detailed analysis of individual works of music. For a supplement to the present book where very few of these analyses could be included, the reader is referred particularly to the two articles in the *Mozart-Jahrbuch* for 1950 and 1951, "Aus der Musiksprache des Mozart-Theaters" and "Zur Musiksprache der Wiener Klassiker" (reprinted as the first two items in Georgiades' *Kleine Schriften*, Tutzing 1977), and to Georgiades' Schubert monograph, *Schubert. Musik und Lyrik* (Göttingen 1967), one chapter of which (analysis of the *Wanderers Nachtlied*) is soon to appear in English translation. Another of Georgiades' main concerns, the changing relationship between notated music and its actual sound, is further explored in his article "Musik und Schrift" (also reprinted in *Kleine Schriften*) and in the volume of essays which he edited, *Musikalische Edition im Wandel des historischen Bewusstseins* (Kassel 1971). For a more detailed presentation of his thoughts on the rhythm of the Greek language the reader may consult Georgiades' *Greek Music, Verse and Dance* in English translation (New York 1956). Georgiades' final work, a book which proceeds from the ideas contained in the last chapter of the present book and entitled *Nennen und Erklingen*, is currently being prepared for posthumous publication.

MLG

1 · Introduction

This book addresses itself to those who are attracted by music, to the friends of music: amateurs as well as professionals. It attempts to focus attention on certain characteristics of the cultural—intellectual sphere which we call music.

If we proceed from our own experience and ask ourselves what we think of as music today, we find that our approach is different from that of our ancestors. For until a short time ago, up to the time of Beethoven or Schubert, the general public's awareness of music was concentrated almost exclusively on contemporary or recently composed works. Since then, however, things have become different; following the Viennese classical period the situation changed abruptly. Mendelssohn, Schumann and Brahms, Berlioz, Liszt and Wagner, and later Richard Strauss — all of these composers did not represent for the public of their own time the musical scene in its entirety. They themselves dedicated a part of their efforts to the interpretation of the music of the past. From that time on it became customary to consider older works just as valid a part of the contemporary scene as those newly composed, and to transmit them accordingly. Thus musical activity in the late nineteenth century was already strongly affected by the past. In the course of the twentieth century the situation has changed ever further to the advantage of older works. Nor does this apply only to the concert hall: activities such as the Youth Movement (Jugendbewegung) and the cultivation of folk song and of amateur chamber-music groups have worked in this direction. And certainly the pursuit of historical research in music has contributed its share. So it is that in the course of the last century and a quarter a fundamental change has occurred in the public consciousness with regard to music; a transformation has taken place in the very concept of music. For the musician and the music-lover of today — even for the composer — new creative work represents only a minor part of what we would call the current musical scene. For in our time works of the past claim the right to be performed; they take their stance as an effective force. The desire to incorporate the music of the past into the consciousness of the present has become so strong that it is no longer possible to speak of an eclectic relationship to certain periods or of the arbitrary singling-

1

out of specific major composers and famous works, or even of a simple longing for that which is past. Our goal is higher: we want to understand music in its entirety as a unified whole — all of the music which lives within us, which has the right to live within us. This, however, is *our* music, that of our own past and present. We are no longer content to accept only those random portions which are readily available to us. It is our ambition to restore all of the components without any gaps and to comprehend the resulting sequence as growth and change. In this totality, this genetically formed unit, we would like to see the very essence of music. In earlier periods music was, for the individual, in a certain sense accidentally determined: it consisted of works currently composed. The concept of music was static; it did not embrace the dimension of growth, of time. It is thus understandable that anyone who reflected on the nature of music, while taking as his point of departure its current and thus accidentally provided segment, soon abandoned this, and with it historical fact in general, to tread the path of pure speculation, as philosopher, in his search for the essence of the musical phenomenon.

How differently is the musical awareness of the present determined! Because music is now understood as a genetic sequence, as an entity, it has taken on the dimension of time. It is no longer possible to ignore this now essential factor. From now on we can make vital observations about music only by pursuing the singular relationship between the permanent and the changing. We soon discover that substance and growth are more closely intertwined than could have been imagined by those of an earlier, more naive and, if one will, more felicitous epoch; that they are inextricably bound one to the other. We perceive that the substance harbors within itself much more of the historical than was formerly suspected, that music can in fact be interpreted only as growth, as change.

It is possible to observe the formation of the music of Western civilization from various angles. Two mutually exclusive viewpoints represent this music (a) as an isolated, aesthetically autonomous phenomenon, as sound, (b) as something rooted in the universal concept of the human—intellectual. The first interpretation can be pursued when attention is focused on the structure of the musical substance. Access to the second is best obtained through an explanation of the relationship between music and language. In this book we propose to do both. We will represent the formation of Western music as the problem of the constant confrontation of music with language; at the same time, however, we will also view music as an autonomous means of expression and will accordingly examine the formation of musical structure.

In a certain sense language stands above art, that is, above poetry or music: as a result of the meaning which it conveys, it expressly points beyond the sphere of the purely aesthetic. It also, however, points to the sound as something constant, as something immutable in its significance. It thus provides a link with the permanent, from which we can measure the changing. Drawing upon language allows the assurance that we can examine change without losing sight of unity.

If, with this in mind, we look for a point of entry into Western music, we find nothing more appropriate than the Mass. With the Mass is linked an entire procession, to this day unbroken, of musical settings of the same text. We are not, however, simply confronted with the connection to language in the strict sense of the word. We are obliged to view music as rooted in the universal domain of the human—historical—intellectual. We touch upon the question of the relationship between idea and music, between event and music. For the language of the Mass is the conveyor of an idea, of an event. By posing the question in this manner we are pursuing as our goal not so much the music itself as the language, the idea, the event as sound. Only when we have succeeded in reversing our point of view, when we have become vitally aware of the secondary position of music with regard to the universal—intellectual on the one hand, while confronting it with the autonomy of musical structure, with the independence of the musical vehicle of meaning on the other — only then can we measure the span between these two cornerstones of musical reality. Only this puts us in a position to understand the phenomenon of music as realized in the formation of Western music in a really comprehensive way.

2
Antiquity and the Pre-Carolingian Period

If we want to understand historical music as a unified whole, we must include antiquity. For present purposes, however, we shall touch only upon those aspects which are necessary in pointing out what it is that connects antiquity and Western civilization and what separates them.

For the ancient Greeks, music existed primarily as verse. The Greek verse line was a linguistic and simultaneously a musical reality. The connecting element, common to both language and music, was rhythm. A verse line in a modern Western language — German, for example — can, to be sure, establish an order in the succession of accents which, proceeding from language, is also binding for the music:

Das Wándern íst des Múllers Lúst.

It cannot, however, by itself determine all aspects of the musical rhythm. For this Western verse line is not a musical but rather a linguistic form. For that reason it can be set to music in various ways:

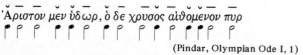

The ancient Greek verse line behaved differently. Here the musical rhythm was contained within the language itself. The musical—rhythmic structure was completely determined by the language. There was no room for an independent musical—rhythmic setting; nothing could be added or changed.

Ἄριστον μὲν ὕδωρ, ὁ δε χρυσος αἰθομενον πυρ

(Pindar, Olympian Ode I, 1)

The ancient Greek word comprised within itself a firm musical component. It had an intrinsic musical will. The individual syllables could be neither extended nor abbreviated. They were by nature long or short. The speaker was obliged to perceive them as stable, inflexible elements. This substantive, concrete aspect of the ancient Greek language was its musically conceived rhythm, and it is precisely this which is missing from modern Western languages.

The essential characteristic of this so-called *quantitative* rhythm lies in the organization of time not by means of the material measure but rather through the utilization of longs and shorts, as they were already contained in the Greek language (see the example above). Time is realized primarily through the almost substantive dimensions of these elements. The demarcation and thus the measurement of time is here the simple result of quantity, of duration. The individual elements do not comply with a pre-existent pattern, with an already organized system of time; rather it is they who, entering as independent quantities, fill in and thus at the same time subdivide the span of time that until then was wholly unarticulated. The rhythmic principle of antiquity is based not on the distinction between the organization of time (the measure, system of accents) and its filling-in (with various note values) but rather on intrinsically filled-in time. This quantitative rhythm was determined by the language; it was a characteristic of the Greek language.

This applies, however, only to the Greek of the ancients. By about the fourth century B.C. a singular process had set in, which can be viewed as the shrinkage of the musical component. This stood in a reciprocal relationship to the modification of the intellectual–cultural outlook of the ancient world. The language became increasingly uncertain in its handling of the musical–rhythmic component, the musical substance became ever less distinct until it vanished altogether. This process was completed during the first centuries of Christendom. But what had become of the firmly structured verse line of ancient Greek? Had it perhaps, after the loss of its musical–rhythmic component, been turned into the kind of verse we know today? By no means. For the verse line of Greek antiquity did not contain even the rudiments of a systematic arrangement of accents; it thus lacked the prerequisite to the formation of the verse of modern Western languages. After the loss of that quality which was essential to the verse, namely its firm rhythmic–musical contour, there remained only a rhythmically amorphous mass. There emerged what we call prose. A reading of the line which we have quoted above without its formerly intrinsic musical rhythm results not in a verse line of the modern Western kind but rather in genuine prose with fortuitous distribution of the accented and unaccented syllables:

Ἄριστον μὲν ὕδωρ, ὁ δὲ χρυσὸς αἰθόμενον πῦρ

As long as the musical–rhythmic principles of antiquity ruled, the accents were performed melodically rather than dynamically. Only after the musical substance had fallen away did they come into the foreground, now transformed into dynamic accents. The succession of accents which resulted does not, however, in any way conform to the rhythmic verse line of antiquity; it is accidental. The verses of modern Western languages are only possible against the background of prose: through the introduction of a system of accents into this rhythmic – let us call it by name – chaos. This process can also be documented historically: whereas we encounter verse (the Homeric hexameter) at the beginning of the ancient Greek linguistic tradition, it is the new prose which we find at the inception of Western Christian history. It is in prose that Christianity is proclaimed, first in Greek, then in Latin; and prose forms the oldest component and the foundation of the Christian liturgy. Verses emerge from this base as a secondary and a later product, and they no longer contain the musical–rhythmic components which characterized the verse of Greek antiquity.

The ancient Greek verse line was a singular formation for which there is no analogy in Western Christian civilization. It was, if you will, music and poetry in one, and precisely because of this it could not be separated into music and poetry as two tangibly distinct components. For this particular vehicle of meaning the Greeks, however, had a special term: μουσική (*musiké*). We thus have the following pattern:

μουσική ⟶ prose ⟶ poetry

(musically determined verse)   (linguistically determined verse)

What, however, has become of the purely musical component of musiké, of the Greek verse line? It appears that in the process of the shrinkage of the linguistic–musical substance there remained, as it were, a musical shell which became autonomous, which became what we call music. We can thus supplement the above diagram as follows:

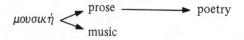

μουσική $\Big<$ prose ⟶ poetry

               music

It is inaccurate to translate *musiké* as *music*, for these two terms designate two different things. *Musiké* cannot be translated; and yet the word lives on to the present time in its Western transformation as *music*, it is on everyone's tongue: and so it is that the etymological identity points to the origin of our music, to the unity of antique and Western civilization, to the intellectual–cultural continuity from Homer to the present day. The change in meaning, however, points to the gulf which separates the two worlds.[1]

From the original unity has resulted a duality; from μουσική have emerged poetry and music. Only now, only within the history of modern Western civilization, has it become possible to separate music and language definitively from one another. From now on there also exists, however, as a reminder, as it were, of their common historical roots, a longing of the one for the other, the tendency to complement each other. The various results of this combination, however, have nothing in common with the musiké of antiquity. For here we are confronted not with an entity which integrates music and language within itself, but rather with a Western language which is expressly set to music.

The tendency towards the combining of language and music is already present in the early Christian liturgy. The linguistic form is prose; it is defined, however, by the necessity to speak in terms of the Cult, in the language of the Christian–sacred community. The Word must sound forth. For within the community the Word exists only in its sounded and not in its written form. As the sacred Word it cannot, however, be made to sound in its natural form as subjectively colored speech. It demands a musically fixed performance. And this is the moment at which Western music is born. The liturgical text forms the portal through which music enters into the cultural history of the Western Christian world.

There begins a constant confrontation between music and the word as the original phenomenon of the intellectual–cultural sphere. This confrontation forms the basis of the history of Western music; it touches the very nerve of its existence.

And what a movement is thus begun! The steadfastness of this confrontation is one of the most impressive features of Western intellectual history. Century after century takes on this task without diminishing its force or interrupting its tradition. The products of the past are transformed, are differently interpreted, and the result is something new. It is within this confrontation that Western music has developed. Well into the seventeenth century, until Heinrich Schütz, the setting of language to music formed the main task of the great historical tradition of music. Only with Bach, in the first half of the eighteenth century, did the focus change. Not that the music which was bound to language now became less important. But in the person of Bach instrumentally conceived music, in a rise of scarcely conceivable rapidity and following approximately a century of preparation, exploited completely new intellectual domains. From this point on it becomes necessary to deal with it specifically, not just for its own sake but also as a means of grasping the new situation of music in general and its new relationship to language in particular.

It is helpful to distinguish among four different periods. The oldest lasts up until Carolingian times. The second begins with the decisive entrance of the Germanic nations into the intellectual—cultural history of the Christian West and ends with the sixteenth century, with the era of the Reformation and the Counter-Reformation, of the Council of Trent and the music of Palestrina. The third begins with Palestrina and ends with the Viennese classical composers, with the death of Beethoven (1827). The fourth extends up to the present time.

The history of Western music forms an entity. The extent to which the various nations participate at any given time within this history, however, varies frequently. For this reason it is necessary to view Europe as a whole and in the course of our representation to direct our gaze in each case to that particular region which calls attention to itself.

In the pre-Carolingian period we are concerned with that part of Europe which lies south of the Alps. Up until the third century the language of the liturgy was Greek, even in Rome, and only after that did Latin take its place. These two languages formed the basis of musical recitation, and they did so as prose, whether the texts resulted from translations (in some cases perhaps even of verse) or were newly written. The realization that it is basically prose which determines the liturgy is, as we have seen above, of primary importance. It indicates a fundamental alteration in the general intellectual—cultural outlook. Only within this new prose did it become possible in European history to differentiate between the poetic—perceptible reality of art on the one hand and religious content as truth on the other, to point to truths which are beyond the reach of sensory perception.

Prose envelops the secret of the transformation in Holy Communion, the center of the Mass. The sacramental words of Christ himself are simple prose, and the same holds true for the other texts which accrued to the liturgy of the Mass: passages from the New Testament, those from the Old Testament (for example psalms, translated as prose), newly written prayers and other texts. Even those chants which were not taken from the Holy Bible, which were new additions, are prose, as we can see in the oldest hymns such as the Gloria in excelsis Deo of the Mass. It is through the intonation of this prose that the sacramental event transpired.

Since Greek liturgical music has its own history as Byzantine church music and did not directly influence the emergence of Western music, we will leave it out of our consideration here. Within the tradition of Latin liturgical chant we do not find ourselves on firm ground until around A.D. 600 with the reign of Pope Gregory the Great, whose name lives on in the term "Gregorian chant." There are, however, clues which make it possible to draw certain conclusions about the form of these chants in even earlier times.

We will take as the basis of our observations the text of the Mass. When we speak of "the Mass" in music, we mean the five chants Kyrie—Gloria—Credo—Sanctus—Agnus, whose texts recur unchanged in every Mass (they comprise the "Ordinary of the Mass"). The texts originated in the first centuries after Christ, but only in the subsequent period did all of these chants gradually become requisite parts of the Mass. To be sure, the history of their musical setting goes back to the origin of the texts, but the transmission of the melodies does not begin until later, until approximately the tenth century. The reason for this may well be the fact that the chants of the Mass belonged intrinsically to the sphere of popular or folk music and thus were not written down at first. For initially they were performed by the congregation, whose place was taken only gradually, towards the end of the first millennium, by the choir of priests and that of the singers.

It should prove helpful to call to mind the change in meaning which the term *choir* has undergone in the course of the centuries. In antiquity — in Homer or in Greek tragedy, for instance — *choir* meant a round-dance with song. In early Christianity it was transferred to the sphere of the celestial: we encounter the "choir of angels" and its earthly counterpart, the choir of priests. The section of the church which corresponds to the latter is known to this day as the "choir." Of equal importance in determining all of these terms, moreover, are the concepts of vocal music on the one hand and of movement on the other. It is the idea of an event taking place in enclosed space. Subsequently the choir of singers disengaged itself from that of the clerics. This brings with it a restriction of the concept in that the idea of movement in space is dropped. Somewhat later the choir of singers even leaves the choir-section and proceeds

to the opposite side of the church, to the gallery, thus emphasizing
its lay character. Finally, we should mention the modern use of the
word "choir" and its derivatives in such terms as "opera chorus" or
"church choir."

The liturgical chant of pre-Carolingian times is characterized by
its monophonic setting. Although our main purpose is to investigate
the emergence of polyphonic music, we will also find it necessary to
form a clear idea of the relationship between music and the Latin
language of monophonic chant. In so doing we will draw on examples
from the chants of the Mass, even though they were not written
down until after the Carolingian epoch, since we wish to lay the
foundations on which we will later build. Older categories of liturgical chant, such as psalmody or the antiphons which surround it,
exhibit the same basic approach to the musical setting of language.

Let us, therefore, examine a setting of the Agnus Dei (the Agnus
of Mass XVIII in the Editio Vaticana): Ex. 1. In translation: "O
lamb of God, who takest away the sins of the world, have mercy
upon us" three times, with the ending *dona nobis pacem* — "grant us
thy peace" — substituted for "have mercy upon us" the third time.

Ex. 1

This text is not declaimed in a natural tone of voice. Use is made
instead of musical pitches. Judged from the standpoint of normal
speaking, this intonation has something unreal about it. Normal
speech, however, would not be appropriate, since the action which
we are describing is not an everyday occurrence, serving practical
purposes. And neither is the word in this case a mere tool of communication. As a result of the musical declamation, however, another
aspect makes its appearance, namely the sacred aspect.

And yet this mode of recitation preserves the character of the
spoken: the sentence can be recognized as a unit, as a meaningful
combination of syntactic elements. We hear the invocation *Agnus*

Dei and its extension *qui tollis peccata mundi*, like an opening, a twice-repeated gesture of prayer; and then the main content of the sentence, namely the petition *miserere nobis*, like a concluding gesture.

Agnus Dei — *qui tollis peccata mundi* — — *miserere nobis*

And this is reflected in the melody, which rests on *a* at the end of each of the first phrases, *Agnus Dei* and *qui tollis*, falling to its close on *g* only at the conclusion of the petition, *miserere nobis*. In its musical recitation, then, which has, compared to a normal speaking tone, something unnatural about it, the text is not rendered incomprehensible, but its liturgical significance is in fact intensified, is brought more plastically into relief.

It is important to remind ourselves that the music does not here capture the content of the language as *meaning*, but rather simply presents the language in its syntactic progression. Only in this sense are we to understand the fact that the phrase *dona nobis pacem* is set to the same melodic formula as *miserere nobis*. The unifying element is the linguistic gesture, the rhythm, not the meaning.

Let us also examine the initial phrases of the Credo (Credo I in the Editio Vaticana), the profession of faith. Here, too, the individual phrases are realized as syntactic units:

Ex. 2

Cre-do in unum Deum,   Pa - trem omni-potentem,   fa - ctorem coeli et ter-rae,

In translation: "I believe in one God, the father almighty, creator of Heaven and earth . . . " In this musical setting, again, the Word retains its immediacy as a living force; it is identical with the liturgical event. Formulated in this way, this appears self-evident. As we will see, however, later epochs approached the liturgical experience from a totally different point of view.

In the example of the Agnus Dei we observed how the musical recitation was governed by the gesture of prayer. One is struck by the spirit of communal action in other chants as well, in the recitation of the litany during processions, for example. The Greek invocation *Kyrie eleison* ("Lord have mercy upon us") was originally just such an entreaty — taken over, initially, from the heathen Cult of the Sun. A report from the sixth century describes how the crowds from seven Roman basilicas thronged praying through the city, "clamantes per plateas urbis Kyrie eleison" ("crying *Kyrie eleison* in the streets"), until they were united in a single litany before the main church of Santa Maria Maggiore.[2]

We find this characteristic of the litany in the Kyrie of the Requiem Mass, which, even though it stems from a later period, still exhibits the older attitude. In the course of a ninefold entreaty (three times *Kyrie eleison*, three times *Christe eleison*, and again three times *Kyrie eleison*) the same melody is sung eight times in the manner of a litany chant — Ex. 3 — to be altered only for the final statement.

The image of the movement of a slowly wandering procession is thus captured.

Ex. 3

Gregorian melodies make use of the diatonic scale: the series of the seven white keys, plus $b\flat$. Characteristic of the individual modes are their range and certain main tones around which the others are grouped. In addition, the particular motives used and the manner in which the main tones are reached are typical of the different melody-types. From the few examples already provided, it is clear that the main tones, that is the central or cadence tones, can vary among the different pieces. The tones *c* and *a*, which would correspond to the tonic notes of the major and minor scales on the white keys, are not typical for Gregorian chants. Gregorian melodies are not built around the more recent major or minor keys, which strive with compelling force towards the tonic. They consist instead of a loose, almost accidental arrangement of tones which is, strictly speaking, valid in each case only for the particular type of melody, for the particular constellation of tones being considered. In the Middle Ages melodies were arranged according to the eight so-called church modes. The main criteria for assigning melodies to one or another of these modes were the cadence tone (finalis), the second most important tone or dominant (repercussa), and the range (ambitus).

It is not possible to answer definitively the question of the historically accurate rhythmic performance of Gregorian chant. In present-day church practice the theory of the Benedictine monks is

widely accepted, according to which all notes have approximately
equal duration. We have also followed this principle in presenting
the Agnus Dei and the beginning of the Credo in the above examples.
But other possibilities are conceivable. Thus equal duration might be
postulated for the individual *syllables* rather than for the individual
tones. The beginning of the Agnus Dei would then read as in Ex. 4.

Ex. 4

This would also correspond well to the state of language at the time
in which the liturgy began to emerge: the shrivelled-up syllables,
which no longer exhibited an independent musical—rhythmic length
(see pp. 5f), can be looked upon as a series of shorts, as elements of
equally short duration. And this came very close to reciting all the
syllables of normal psalmody in equal short values — for example, as
simple eighth-notes. When brief embellishments occurred, they were
interpreted as rhythmic subdivisions of these short syllabic units (see
the two sixteenth-notes on the syllable *De-* in the last example). By
extending this principle it is possible to regulate the temporal progression even of those melodies which are not strictly syllabic —
melismatic chants — in a constant alternation of stress and release, so
that in the distribution of notes different rhythmic values emerge.
The rhythm of the processional Kyrie from the Requiem Mass was
determined according to this principle (Ex. 3 above).

    In the tenth century it became customary to underlay the
melismas of the chant with a text which functioned as a kind of
interpretation or paraphrase of the original liturgical text. As an
example let us take the Kyrie of Mass IV in the Editio Vaticana, in
which the word *Kyrie* was replaced by the text

    (Kyrie   ˘ _   ˘ ˘ _ D˘˘ _ ˘ĭc˘˘ _   eleison)
    Cunctĭpŏtens genĭtor Deŭs omnĭcrĕātor eleison

("Omnipotent God, Father, Creator of all things, have mercy upon
us"). This line (omitting the *eleison*) forms a verse based upon an
antique model, a dactylic pentameter. In cases such as this, then, we
are presented with yet a further possibility in determining the
rhythm of Gregorian chant. It is conceivable that the melody was
performed rhythmically, as shown in Ex. 5. The practice of creating
new, secondary texts of this kind emerges, however, only in

Ex. 5

Cun - cti-potens ge - ni-tor De-us o - mnicre-a - tor   e · · · · · le - i-son.

Carolingian times, and specifically in the region north of the Alps. It touches upon questions belonging to the next chapter.

3 · The Carolingian Period

These new accessories which we have just mentioned above, these secondary liturgical components which arose in connection with a main liturgical chant, are called tropes. In all probability there were also tropes which took as their basis secular rather than liturgical melodies. In this way the pre-Christian musical heritage of the Northern peoples may well have found its way into the church. This constituted an enrichment of Western music. Initially, the tropes were written either as prose or, as in the example quoted above, in verses composed on antique models. Only from the eleventh century onward did rhymed verses come into the foreground. In later times some of the tropes detached themselves from their original surroundings and lived on as independent sacred songs. It is along this path that the German language gained entrance to the liturgy in the Middle Ages, and it did so in the form of verse. (The vernacular was thus admitted to the church (a) not at the primary liturgical level but rather in the form of these subsidiary texts, and (b) not as prose, like the primary liturgical layer, but rather in the form of verses. It is important to keep these two statements in mind if we are to understand properly the German liturgy with which we will concern ourselves later.)

"Trope" is a word of Greek origin (*trópos*), where it means "manner," in the sense of the way or fashion of doing something (particularly in its application to music). The term "trope" can therefore be understood as interpretation, as paraphrase of the primary liturgical text. In Byzantine church music the word, in the form *troparion*, took on the meaning of church song. This is analogous to the German word *Weise*, meaning melody or song. In an expression such as "Vortragsweise" the relationship of the two meanings can be observed: the manner or method of performance — that is, *how* the text is made to sound — and at the same time the melody itself, the "Weise," to which the text is sung. In this way the term "trope," which designates the new type of text, also sheds light on the liturgical function of the music: music is not an end in itself but rather the manner in which the sacred texts are recited.

The texts of the tropes were created out of a desire to interpret and supplement the main liturgical text. Thus the phrase *Cunctipotens genitor Deus omnicreator* took the place of the simple *Kyrie*. The primary, consecrated liturgical text was considered inviolable, as dogma, as it were. It has also been assumed, as a result, that the primary liturgical text (in this case *Kyrie eleison*) and its trope sounded simultaneously — that, for example, one half of the choir recited the trope while the other half sang the untroped text.

Let us attempt to reconstruct such a performance. In Byzantine church music, in the Greek Orthodox Church, it is a common practice to this day to reinforce the given melody with sustained tones, by means of a so-called bourdon accompaniment. It is quite conceivable that something similar took place in the West during the Carolingian period. Let us apply this to the Kyrie Cunctipotens by letting the main liturgical text and its trope be performed by two different groups: the singers who are responsible for the realization of the stationary voice, the bourdon, enter with the word *Kyrie* and hold this tone while the chant, with the verses of the trope *Cunctipotens*, is sung. The two groups of singers do not join forces until the word *eleison*, which they perform together:

Ex. 6

In a recitation of this kind we remove ourselves from the sphere of normal speaking, and yet in a certain sense we come closer to the real significance of speech. By means of the main tone, which sounds continuously, the language is embedded in a single sound. Thus it is present not only as a combination of phrases, as in the monophonic Gregorian version, but in addition to this as a continuous flow, as a unit of meaning which cannot be broken up into separate elements.

A single sphere of sound is established, which is not interrupted and which holds together the course of events in the language. In this way the spoken word takes on an aspect of the inviolable: it is removed from the sphere of arbitrary action.

A performance of this sort, however, comes close to polyphony. And indeed it seems natural to connect the simultaneous recitation of a main text and its paraphrase, this singular — let us say — poly-textuality with its musical analogue, polyphony. It is possible, then, to comprehend the emergence of polyphony from the standpoint of a theological–liturgical requirement: the need to present the hallowed text and its interpretative paraphrase simultaneously. One could also view polyphony as a kind of *musical* paraphrase of the given mono-phonic liturgical melody. Trope and liturgical polyphony thus have a similar perceptual outlook: both bring forth something new without excluding the old, the liturgical foundation. On the contrary the new is itself sanctified in that it utilizes the old and builds on it. Thus, the liturgical melody was also held sacred, in the manner of a dogma. Carolingian polyphony is nothing more than a particular way of per-forming the given monophonic liturgical chant.

The supposition that the introduction of a polyphonic manner of performing the liturgical chant is related to the tropes is also sub-stantiated historically. Not only do both of these phenomena first confront us at the same time and in the same region, in the ninth century north of the Alps, but the sources which report to us about the oldest polyphonic rendition of liturgical chant illustrate this polyphony with examples of tropes (specifically, with sequences, a category of trope applied to the Alleluia chants).

With this first historically tangible polyphony we find ourselves facing the impressive beginnings of Western music in its strict sense.

The main source is the *Musica Enchiriadis*, a theoretical music treatise from the second half of the ninth century which was dis-tributed in numerous manuscripts over all of Europe, from England and France, Belgium and Germany to Spain, Italy and Austria.[3] This wide distribution is in itself evidence of the high esteem in which the work was held. One of its sections deals with the polyphonic per-formance of a Gregorian melody. This is given the name *Organum*. The author uses the melody *Rex coeli* (see Ex. 7) as "vox principalis," the given chant.

This chant is now provided with a sonorous foundation of singular type. As long as the melody moves within the range $c-a$, this sup-porting voice, the "vox organalis," employs the tones $c-e$. The tones *f-g-a* in the melody are joined in each case by the lower fourth (*c-d-e*). Since the vox organalis may not descend lower than *c*, however, it is obliged, whenever the melody descends below *f*, either to remain on *c* or to move in unison with the melody. When the latter, on the other hand, leaves the range *c–a* and ascends above it, the supporting voice is transposed up a fifth so that it now responds to the notes *g–e'* in the melody with *g–b*. The organal performance of the given chant thus takes on the form shown in Ex. 7.[4]

Ex. 7

This method of recitation must not be regarded as an independently composed polyphonic work. Anyone who mastered the rules could perform liturgical chant in this manner as improvisation. The individual piece was not the result of creative accomplishment in the sense in which we usually associate it with the idea of the finished composition, the independent work of art. Organum was regarded simply as a way of performing liturgical chant. It is thus more closely related to an improvised bourdon accompaniment (see above) than it is to the concept of the finished composition. Organum, too, is the result of embedding the word in sound.

And yet, in a very important sense, organum cannot be compared to that foundation provided by a stationary tone. There the bourdon tone was the main tone of the melody, the finalis *d*. As a result the melodic character of the chant, its musical principle of unity, its original structure were not in the least impaired; on the contrary, these characteristics were brought more into the foreground. In the organum, however, it is the concept of the vertical consonance which prevails. The sonorous element takes over with a will of its own which alters fundamentally the original significance of the given chant. Without regard for the finalis and the other main notes of the melody (see above), any chant can be relegated, mechanically if you will, to the compartments of sound outlined above. In order to specify range from that vantage point it is not necessary to ask, for example, whether the melody closes on *c* or *d* or *e*. The new con-

cept of vertical sound is so powerful that — as we will soon see — it
actually modifies the original chants.

How can this technique be described, and what are its characteristics? In the form of a diagram it might be represented as in Ex. 8a.

When the chant contains bb, it is appropriate to encompass it
within the limits shown in Ex. 8b.

Ex. 8a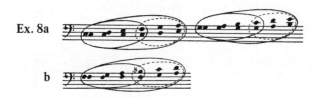

b

Enclosed compartments of sound are formed, whose perimeters
are determined by the range of a sixth (c–a or g–e). A compartment
of this kind is a unit; it rests within itself. One cannot break through
its boundaries. An extension of the range c–a, however, to include
the b or bb either above or below would have the effect of a per-
foration, would mean just such a rupture of the sound unit. When
the melody extends beyond the range c–a, therefore, it must also
abandon that particular compartment of sound and take on a new
one. The original sound complex cannot be made to expand or move
forward in conformity with the flow of the melody. It is, as it were,
rooted to the spot; its character is static. Nor can it be divided into
separate consonances. What is encompassed within its limits must be
understood as an indivisible unit. Thus we have before us not the
sum of separate sonorities, of unisons, seconds, thirds and fourths,
but rather a single concept of sound, which expresses itself in a certain way, as a rotating movement of the tones.

This enclosed compartment of sound is characterized by three
features: (a) the fourth-structure, (b) the range of a sixth, (c) the
major scale. Let us consider it more closely. The Greeks also took
the fourth as their point of departure. They employed it mainly as a
melodic interval. In the *Musica Enchiriadis*, however, it is given a
new meaning: it is used as a consonance. For the melody notes c to f
it appears as the end consonance towards which the movement is
aimed: Ex. 9a. Here it is also effective as melody, for the melody
tones c to f pass through the interval of a fourth. From that point on
the vertical structure of sound changes. There appear only fourth-
consonances: Ex. 9b. If we attempt to sing these fourths in succession

slowly, we find them completely strange to our ears. For from the later music with which we are well acquainted we know the fourth not as a self-contained sonority, but rather as either the suspension to the third — Ex. 9c — or the inversion of the fifth — Ex. 9d. The

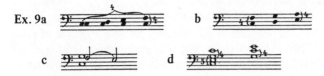

Ex. 9a   b

c   d

fifth and the third incorporate for us the qualities of the approachable, the friendly, the variable, the sociable. They like to form combinations. The fifth is divisible into two mutually friendly if not exactly equal sonorities, the major and minor third; two thirds form a fifth. Nothing of this sort applies to the fourth. It is complete within itself, which however means closed off, sphinxlike, muffled, compact.

And thus it is that a musical culture such as that of ancient Greece, which was based on the fourth, is very difficult for us to comprehend. The music of the Carolingian period also takes the fourth as its point of departure; but the exaggeration of the principle leads to its downfall. The fourth appears here both as melodic interval and as vertical sonority, a fact which has consequences for the organization of the sound complex. This is fashioned around the core of the melodically unfolding fourth, which thus transforms itself into a sonority (see above, Ex. 9a). This sonority of the fourth begins to move in its turn, and stretches the sound core as far as it can go (see above, Ex. 9b). The sixth is reached, and this represents the boundary. For beyond this emerges the dreaded gap caused by the diffuse, indeterminate tone *b/bb* (or *f/f♯*). With that, however, the major scale *c-d-e-f-g-a* appears of its own accord. The ambitus of the sixth that results cannot be derived from the church modes of Gregorian chant (e.g. Dorian *d-e-f-g-a-b*). The loose framework of the Gregorian church modes here becomes secondary to the concept of sonority and to the major scale resulting from it. One could even say that the modal framework is abrogated by the new structural quality of the sixth.

Thus this determined will of the fourth to extend itself leads to emancipation from its own single domination and to the vanquishment of the church modes (see also p. 17). For the newly created compartment of sound is determined by the compass of a sixth, by the *hexachord*, and in fact by the hexachord as a major scale. In addition the two hexachord compartments *c–a* and *g–e'* stand in a fifth-relationship to one another: *g–e'* is the transposition of *c–a* a fifth upward. It is by the force of these new elements that the formation of polyphony is set in motion.

To be sure, the polarity of two tones in a fifth-relationship to one another and the ambitus of a hexachord are also effective to some extent within Gregorian chant, but only melodically; lacking in this case are both the singular, structural relationship of the fourth and the exclusive, compelling realization of the hexachord as the major scale. Only in polyphony, in the *Musica Enchiriadis*, are we confronted with these new aspects. The Carolingian age and the *Musica Enchiriadis*, to be sure, consider themselves traditionally oriented. By starting with the fourth, they imagine themselves to be building on the heritage of Greek music. And precisely because of this they create something entirely new. This was only possible, however, because they combined the principle of the tetrachord — that mere skeleton which had come down to them from the distant past as an abstract intellectual remnant — with their own immediate musical reality, the fundamental musical powers of the new races north of the Alps.

There is reason to believe that these pagan Germanic peoples were familiar with a music inherently different from that of Southern Europe. They based their experience on the sonority and on group instrumental playing, not on the cantilena or on song. Their music was founded on a principle of vertical sonority rather than on one of melodic linearity.[5] There was a tendency towards chordal blocks of sound, which, simply by virtue of the number and type of instruments involved (probably brass or gong-like instruments), appeared ponderous, unwieldy and therefore phlegmatic. Sonorities of a static nature such as the fourth or even the second were given preference, as were doublings at the octave, which filled out a great expanse of sound. Sonorities of this kind did not move forward melodically, but rather swung vibrating on their own axes, circumscribed by ornamental figures. They functioned like ringing bells. Let us take a hypothetical example as an aid in directing our imagination down this path: Ex. 10. Here, too, a certain impression of major establishes itself, the major scale *c-d-e-f-g-a* (the third *e* being omitted).

The organum of the *Musica Enchiriadis* is founded on this approach to music. The term itself points to the instrumental origin,

Ex. 10

the instrumental idea (Greek–Latin *Organum* = "instrument"). But the technique of doubling is also specifically described. In the *Musica Enchiriadis* we even find the chant treated in a manner which consists solely of doublings of the given melody at the fifth and the octave: Ex. 11. The text also mentions the use of doublings to cover a range of three octaves (including instruments). A sound volume of this size was not easily moved. Thus we find the assertion that organum was performed "cum modesto morositate," with deliberate slowness.

Ex. 11

Sit glo-ri-a do-mi-ni in sae-cu-la,lae-ta-bi-tur do-mi-nus in o-pe-ri-bus su-is.

The musical concept of the Germanic peoples is, as we have shown, mirrored in organum. But it would be beyond our reach, it would mean nothing to us, had not the encounter with the word taken place. Only through the word, as the active memory of Western civilization, did Germanic music gain an influence on European history. Only the coupling of Germanic music, that nameless unknown x, with the Christian word as it sounded in music brought about the transformation of this potential musical design into Western intellectual reality and laid the foundation for the music which was to come. There was an obsessive urge to create a unity out of these seemingly irreconcilable approaches to music, the Germanic in the north and the Christian in the south. And thus emerged Western polyphonic music.

But this new music was also substantially determined by the encounter between the Nordic concept of *language* and that of the South. We assumed earlier (see p. 15) that the performance of a trope was accompanied by the simultaneous recitation of the untroped primary liturgical text. A performance of this kind does not, to be sure, conform to our natural feeling for language. This trait, this un-natural speaking, is further strengthened by the metrical presentation of the text:

Cun-ctipo-tens geni-tor Deus o-mnicre-a-tor.

The natural flow of the language, the speech gesture, is here lost. It is as if it had suddenly been discovered that the individual syllables have a weight of their own, that the sentence can be dissected into independent syllables. It is evident that the discovery of this aspect of language, which from now on holds the foreground, is related to the employment of texts in verse-form. We also observed, however, that this new trend which emerges in the Carolingian age, this tendency towards interpretative paraphrase of the basic text, was consummated north of the Alps. Through the propagation of Christianity the Latin liturgical language came into contact with Germanic languages. Thus we can also assume that the awakening of a feeling for the weight of the individual syllables in the recitation of Latin was prompted by this contact with languages which, in contrast to the Latin south of the Alps, had a ponderous, chopped-up sound.

This tendency, moreover, was also encouraged — in fact very strongly supported — by the musical attitudes characteristic of the regions north of the Alps and by the independent weight of the vertical sonorities. The phlegmatic character of these sounds was transferred to the recitation of the text; the chordal ideal retarded the flow of language. To each syllable was attached a sonority. A process was thus initiated which resulted, in the course of the tenth and eleventh centuries, in the isolation and autonomy of the individual syllables. Because of this the intact sound compartments of the *Musica Enchiriadis* could disintegrate in later times into separate sonorities.

The thrust of Christianity to the North resulted in the dissolution of the linguistic unit by the music. The language no longer resounded as a cohesive unit of meaning, as an entire sentence, as a gesture of speech. It was as though frozen, and it broke apart into separate syllables. The task now was to join these syllables in a new manner and thus to construct a whole, to create — differently than in the first thousand years — the linguistic reality anew *from the music.*

What is the significance of this conception of music in the Carolingian era? How does it illuminate the liturgical event? In the course of its conversion to Christianity the North assimilated the liturgical texts with their traditional melodies. For it was necessary that the language should be taken over as the language of the congregation, as liturgy and thus as something which can be perceived, which sounds forth. The musical setting of the texts had, however, to be adapted to the attitude to music held by the new peoples. And with that the earlier manner of performance was turned into its exact opposite: the language is no longer directly accessible to the senses. It exists, as it were, only as dogma; it is only conceptually present.

A deep division thus separates the newly emerging music from Gregorian chant, a division characterized not only by the abandonment of monophonic performance, nor only by the dissection of the language into syllables of independent weight: in addition to this, the liturgy and therefore the religious content are no longer experienced as a living presence through the language but rather as valid dogma, as something which was established in a series of events beyond our comprehension at a faraway place and a remote point in time. Only now can we draw a clear distinction between the given fact of Christianity and the manner of its historical realization. And this is the beginning of the Middle Ages.

This means that the new music, which is based on the sonority, must always employ the given Gregorian melody as its foundation. It is nothing more than a paraphrase of this given *cantus firmus*, this fixed chant.

In the Carolingian era three heterogeneous musical factors come together: (a) a factor that is historical in the strict sense, namely the musical heritage of the Greeks as it emerged from theoretical reflection; (b) Christian music as it was formed by historical continuity, that is, the Roman and also the Byzantine tradition familiar to the *Musica Enchiriadis*; (c) the music of the pagan Germanic peoples which lay beyond the limits of the European historical stream of events. The single element which fused these factors into a unit signifying something new, which established an intellectual continuity in music from antiquity to the New Age, was the power of the Word, the resounding Christian Word.

4 · The High Middle Ages

The Kyrie trope *Cunctipotens* has come down to us in an organum version from around 1100 (in the so-called Milan treatise,[6] – that is, as in the case of the *Musica Enchiriadis*, in a theoretical work: not as a composition in the strict sense of the word, but rather as an example of the organal treatment of a cantus firmus – see p. 17): Ex. 12. Whereas the organum in the *Micrologus* of Guido of Arezzo, from the beginning of the eleventh century, was essentially the same as that of the *Musica Enchiriadis*,[7] the example given here exhibits a completely new approach to the cantus firmus. The process of slowing down the individual sonorities and thus of rendering them independent is already so far advanced that we find only an occasional reminiscence of that unified sound compartment of the hexachord

Ex. 12

Cun · cti · po · tens ge · ni · tor De · us o · mni · cre · a · tor

which originally held them together (for example, the passage *genitor deus*). The relationship to the given liturgical chant has also been altered as a result. In the *Musica Enchiriadis* the liturgical melody was simply supported by a sonority, embedded in a sonority. It had not lost its melodic nature entirely. Here, however, it disintegrates into separate tones, each of which forms the basis of an independent sonority. As a result, the original chant is no longer directly comprehensible to the senses as a recognizable melody. It is employed instead as a structural foundation of sound and has thus been transferred from the upper to the lower voice. From now on it is present only in the abstract, as a rigidified cantus firmus. As consonances we find the unison, the fourth, the octave and, with increasing frequency from now on, the fifth. It is as if the two types of organum described in the *Musica Enchiriadis* had come together in this new version: the genuine organum built around the fourth, and the mere reinforcement of the liturgical chant by means of doublings at the fifth and the octave. In this new organum as well, the individual sonorities probably acquired a large sound volume: they filled in a

broad spectrum of sound through the employment of doublings at
both higher and lower octaves, achieved with the aid of boys' voices
and instruments. The independent weight of the individual sonority
was further increased by the tendency to dwell on it at some length
and to improvise ornaments around it. For the sonority of that time
cannot be identified with the modern "chord." It could not be held
over a longer period of time in unchanged form, but rather functioned
within time as movement; it was active. A practical set of rules for
this improvised art of ornamentation, illustrated with an almost
boundless profusion of examples, is to be found in the so-called
Vatican Organum Treatise, a theoretical work of the twelfth century.[8] If we apply these rules to the first sonorities of the organum
Cunctipotens, here notated only in skeletal form, while at the same
time drawing upon instruments and doublings, we should gain some
insight into the method of converting that mute notation into live,
resounding music:

Ex. 13

The process by which the sonorities became autonomous also
brought with it, however, an awareness of the need to link them
together. The dissolution of the idea of the enclosed sound compartment, as present in the *Musica Enchiriadis*, in favor of individual
sonorities raised the necessity of finding new criteria for their
succession. In moving on to the next tone of the cantus firmus it
was necessary to decide which sonority to employ. In the case of

stepwise movement in the cantus firmus preference was often given
to repetition, for example of fourths (as on *(ge)nitor De(us)*) or of
fifths. Otherwise an attempt was made to change the quality of
sound, and here the progression of the various sound components in
contrary motion became particularly important (as on *(Cun)ctipo-
(tens)*). In the first case the sonorities were merely placed next to
one another; in the second, there arose something akin to an affiliation, a genuine connection.

At this point it also becomes necessary to anchor these sonorities by means of notation. For this music is no longer, as in the
Musica Enchiriadis, merely a manner of performing the chant which
results from the application of the rules (see pp. 17 and 24), but
rather in each case a specific individual realization, a *res facta*, a
finished work. The musician sorts out and combines the sonorities
with a free hand, he com-poses. Only from this point on can we
speak of polyphonic composition in the strict sense of the word.
And accordingly we now find collections of organum-compositions:
following initial attempts in England as early as the eleventh century,
large collections make their appearance in the twelfth century in
Northern Spain and especially in France (St. Martial). Similarly, the
ornamental figures, which as we observed were formerly a question
of performance, are now at least partially written out. They thus
detach themselves from the level of improvisation and become
instead an integral part of the res facta.

From this evidence we can conclude: what is notated is looked
upon as the result of composition in the narrower sense; what
remains at the level of performance practice is not preserved in
writing. Thus notation is the partner of that aspect of music which is
thought to be composition, that is, the accomplishment of the composer; it is not identical with the actual sound, with that which we
are wont to call music. For precisely those elements which make
music what it is, which determine the sound itself — the possibilities
of ornamentation, doublings, mode of performance (whether purely
vocal or with instruments, soloistic or choral, employing men's
voices alone or men's and boys' voices together), tempo, variations
in volume, quality of sound — all of these cannot be deduced from
the notation. Even the precise quality of the intervals is not revealed
in notation. How a second or a third was constituted acoustically, its
actual frequency relationship, is something which we learn only
through familiarity with the tonal system. Thus, the decipherment
of the notation is not identical with the re-creation of the music. A

gulf lies between notation and music as sound. The same applies also to later music — indeed to all music which is transmitted through notation, even when it has been written down in a form much more complete than that of the Middle Ages.

This characteristic, then, is peculiar to the discipline of music history, namely that the subject with which it concerns itself, the music, is not present in finished form. It must first be created. For this reason the essence of interpretation in music history should lie in the *making* of music, the demonstration of the way in which sound can be brought forth. This can only be suggested, however, through the use of sound recordings. Unless musicology employs recordings for this specific purpose, it will not be able to find a method appropriate to its investigation. Recordings should be employed as a means of calling attention to the problematic nature of the subject, of pointing emphatically to the difficulty of repro- ducing music and to the relationship between notation and sound, and not — as so often happens — of providing ready-made music as illustration of a text, as music history in examples. For when music history functions in this manner, it commits the error of assuming that the object of its investigation is present in the same sense as that of the history of art or of the history of literature. To present music as a finished product, as an example, is to set something arbitrary, something which is not binding, in place of the historical reality — unless, of course, we propose to make the particular interpretation itself the object of our investigation. But with that we will have to leave for the moment the question of the relationship between notation and sound.[9]

Through the elaboration of a cantus firmus into a distinct com- position polyphonic music began to appear as something autonomous, as an end in itself. There arose a tendency to look upon it as an interlude, as an insertion into the liturgy. The way to this develop- ment had, however, already been prepared by the previous history of organum. As we have seen, it was the tropes, those chants which originated as subordinate insertions or paraphrases, which provided the opening for polyphonic performance of the chant. In the period following 1100 this characteristic of an insertion now becomes even more prominent in conjunction with the emergence of notated com- positions. For from now on until well into the fourteenth century the polyphonic setting of chants from the Ordinary of the Mass (see p. 9) subsides completely, and a special category of chant is given preference in polyphonic treatment, a category which had from the very beginning fulfilled a specifically musical function. These are the chants which are interpolated between the lessons (Epistle and Gospel), that is the Gradual and the Alleluia jubilus. Here there were frequent melismas, and the syllables were spread far apart. Since the concern was thus not primarily with a musical realization of the *language*, there came into being an independent musical activity. It was an event worth noting when the singer, whose name was announced in the presence of the Pope, mounted the steps of the ambo to sing the Gradual. He was followed by another, the singer of the Alleluia. These chants, then, had the character of an interlude from the very beginning; they were genuine (and in fact quite long) musical insertions between the lessons.

A comparison with the plastic arts can perhaps serve to illuminate the difference between the two types of chant. Those chants in which language, that is the text, comes to the fore are like a realization of man as a speaking creature. Here language is the given element. It is just as essential to an understanding of the musical work as is the representation of the human form to the plastic arts. And just as it is not possible to look solely at colors and forms without considering their relationship to the person portrayed, so it is also necessary to set the tones in relationship to the text which is presented. The melismatic chants and, particularly after around 1100, their polyphonic settings can, on the other hand, best be compared to *ornament* in the plastic arts — to ornament as an independent expression of art. Now it became important, proceeding from this mosaic-like combination of melodic motives and sonorities, to recapture man as a creature of language, to create him anew from this perspective; it became important to find a synthesis between the two categories, between ornament and human portrayal. And this became the task of Western music: the "musical realization" of language or, if you will, the linguistic realization of music, a process which bears witness to a deep insight into the significance of the task. This process extended with unwavering consistency over a period of almost a thousand years, until it reached its climax in Viennese classical music, with Haydn, Mozart, and Beethoven. Its goal was music as the representation of man in the sense of his likeness to God.

The period around 1100, then, provides a caesura. The result of the establishment of the instrumental-sonority principle only now appears to take effect (see p. 20): the transition from the art category of human portrayal as the realization of language to that of ornament.

And this may explain why, as long as polyphony remained at this level, that particular category of liturgical chant was cultivated which could be termed musical interlude, and why the polyphonic setting of the Ordinary of the Mass was not taken up again until the fourteenth century.

In the meantime musical practice turned during the thirteenth century to other tasks. Around 1200 the Notre Dame School reached its zenith under Magister Perotin. Here originated the great organa which were notated for three and even four voices. These notated sonorities, however, took on now, as they had done earlier, a much larger volume by virtue of doublings and the employment of instruments.

They were notated for three or four voices because the individual sonorities now consisted of various different tones rather than only of two, as had formerly been the case. In earlier times one employed only two-note sonorities (such as Ex. 14a), whereas now three- or even four-note sonorities became the rule (as in Ex. 14b or 14c).

Ex. 14a   b   c

It is probably this impact of the sonorous element which necessitated a more consciously developed system of rhythmic articulation than had previously been known. An impetus was provided by the desire for a recurring stress at regular intervals, similar to the regularly repeated impact of the blow of the hammer. There materialized during the performance of an organum steadily recurring rhythmic patterns, the so-called rhythmic modes, for example:

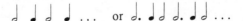

Modal rhythm, however, soon joined forces with a new level of the musical realization of language. In the course of the thirteenth century there emerged from organum the motet: the textless series of sonorities which formed the organum, the original melismas, were underlaid with new texts — a technique reminiscent of the trope. New voices were also added. In later times different texts were applied to each of the individual voices. In a performance these were sung simultaneously, and in fact together with the text syllables of the cantus firmus.[10]

Soon we find not only multi-texted but also multi-lingual motets

(Latin and French, for example). It was even possible to combine sacred and secular texts, but in a manner whereby the idea repre- sented by the cantus-firmus text could function as a common link.

Does this not, however, come close to a ravishment of language? Inasmuch as we look upon language as coherent meaning, it does indeed. The essential element of language does not make itself felt. But through the music other aspects are brought to the fore. What had begun with the organum of the Carolingian period is here brought to its logical conclusion; what had there remained latent is here given specific form. The sheer substantive rhythmic impact of the language is here made manifest through the music — a trait which is related to the Germanic conception of music (see pp. 21f). The inflexibility, however, which results particularly from the employment of the schematic rhythmic modes permits us to become cognizant of yet another aspect of language. Instead of the vital continuity of meaning it is now the schematic—symbolic relationship to an external idea, to the cantus firmus, which becomes prominent. This, too, is a trait of the Germanic spirit, and one which we have already encountered in the liturgical application of Gregorian chant, beginning with the Carolingian era but in particular from around 1100 onward (see pp. 14 and 23). We can see that the thirteenth century is still far removed from a musical realization of language in all its aspects. Nonetheless it calls our attention through its music to specific characteristics and thus provides certain prerequisites for subsequent stages in the musical setting of language.

Modal rhythm, to be sure, represents language as something rigid. By regulating the flow into systematic rhythmic patterns, however, it also offers the first possibility of subdividing the language — albeit mechanically — and, through repetition of the rhythmic patterns, of presenting it in continuity.

This is also, however, facilitated by the transformation of the musical structure: in the course of the thirteenth century there came to the fore one particular triad, namely that one which today bears the name "triad" exclusively. It consists of two thirds which together build a fifth: major plus minor third, *c-e-g*, or minor plus major third, *a-c-e*. With this, however, musical syntax is guided into new paths. Until now fourths and fifths had provided the foundation of the sonorities. These intervals could not, however, enter into close affiliation — an affiliation, that is, which forms a new unit with a character of its own. This is only made possible through the new prominence of the third. Third and fifth complement each other in

a singular manner. They unite with each other to form a new configuration, the triad. And what, we may ask, are its characteristics?
Repose, and yet at the same time a tendency towards movement,
towards combination and advancement. The immobile, static character comes to the triad through the fifth; the agreeable quality associated with it, through the rounding-off which results from the combination of two thirds to form a fifth. The tendency towards
movement, on the other hand, is passed on to the triad by the third.
There are no perfect, self-sufficient thirds, in analogy to a perfect
fourth or fifth, but only major or minor thirds (in other musical
cultures they are differentiated even further). The interval of a third
does not rest in itself; rather, it strives towards a static sonority,
towards resolution in a perfect, unambiguous interval. The components of the third lead the way to this concluding sonority. The
major third tends towards the fifth (Ex. 15a), the minor third
towards the unison (Ex. 15b).

Ex. 15a b

Through the triad, then, the linear--melodic inclination towards
movement was superimposed on the static concept of music built
around sonorities. (In the thirteenth century the triad's need for
movement was felt more strongly than its stationary quality, for this
was the new characteristic. As a result, fifths and octaves without
thirds were long retained as the sole cadential consonances.) Only at
this point did music come into possession of the prerequisites for
polyphony in its true sense, in which both the urgent tendency
towards forward movement and the primarily sonorous element are
inherently contained, a polyphony whose sounds can form a compelling cohesiveness, a unified flow. (But in the thirteenth century
we find only the prerequisites to this change. It was to be a long
time before all the consequences were realized.)

It is understandable that the new tendency should also have its
effects on the realization of language: only now did polyphonic
music acquire the means which permitted it to realize language as
continuity, as continuous flow, to attempt something similar to the
monophonic Gregorian chant of the first millennium, to take up
once again the task of representing man as a speaking being.

It has been assumed that there was in England a particular preference for thirds from earliest times. In the fourteenth century this led

— as we will see in the next chapter — to the emergence of a new,
flowing musical format. It may, however, be appropriate to combine
this observation with the striking fact that it is precisely in England
that we find at this same time polyphonic Mass compositions in
which the flow of the language is given expression.

5
The Fourteenth and Fifteenth Centuries

Before we investigate the English practice, however, let us direct our
attention to the Continent. Whereas Italy's contribution during the
fourteenth century was limited to secular polyphony, there have
come down to us from the French-speaking sphere two complete
Masses (see p. 9) — the oldest known — namely the so-called Mass
of Tournai and the Mass setting by Machaut.

The older of the two is the Mass of Tournai,[11] named after the
Belgian city of Tournai, where the manuscript containing the composition is preserved. The Mass is written for three voices and can
probably be dated in the first half of the fourteenth century. The
Kyrie, Sanctus and Agnus are set in a more archaic fashion than the
Gloria and Credo. The weight of the individual sonorities, which is
here still crucial, produces a metrically vigorous delivery. The Gloria
and Credo are, in contrast, more mobile with respect both to rhythm
and to sonorities. Modal rhythm has been abandoned. In the Gloria
the two upper voices in particular move frequently in smaller note

Ex. 16

values. Here we are not so clearly aware of a metrical pattern; the music flows more freely, and it becomes possible to take the language into consideration as connected prose: Ex. 16.

The Mass of Machaut did not originate until the second half of the fourteenth century: it may have been composed for the coronation of the French King Charles the Fifth, in the year 1364. The poet and musician Guillaume de Machaut is the most important composer of the fourteenth century. His Mass is notated for four voices — an unusual case, since compositions of the fourteenth century are generally written for no more than three voices. The Kyrie is based on the cantus firmus Kyrie *Cunctipotens* which we have discussed above; Sanctus and Agnus employ as cantus firmus the corresponding chants from the Gregorian Mass XVII. When these movements are performed, however, the cantus firmus can scarcely be detected amid the framework of sonorities. Its mere presence was enough to satisfy the demands of religion and liturgy. Gloria and Credo do not employ a cantus firmus.

In this Mass we perceive a tendency to bunch the syllables together into phrases (see Ex. 36, p. 67 below). Within these phrases, however, mechanical scansion is still the rule, resulting among other things in the improper accentuation of individual syllables. The structural—schematic quality of Machaut's motets, then, is also characteristic of his Mass. The techniques which had been acquired from organum to motet are now applied to the composition of the Mass, to the first stages of a new kind of encounter with the primarily liturgical Word of the Mass text.

These Masses differ, however, only slightly from other musical activity of the time, which in the fourteenth century was oriented essentially towards the secular. A secular tendency made itself felt in the liturgy, too, simply by the fact that priests and singers now became independent of one another. Whereas on the one hand the priest now became solely responsible for the recitation of the liturgy in the so-called "missa lecta" (the silent Mass), the musical Ordinary of the Mass achieved independence on the other hand as the only audibly sounding agent of the sacred service. With that the weight of the liturgical action shifted decisively to the musical side. From now on it is possible to regard the Mass as an independent musical work of art. Thus the new phase of the musical composition of the Mass begins with a victory for the independence of polyphonic music. The characteristics which we identified in the twelfth and thirteenth centuries — namely the domination of polyphony by the category of independent musical insertion, by music as ornament – find their parallel here.

We have already mentioned that the cultivation of polyphonic sacred music declined during the fourteenth century. Only England constitutes an exception, and it is here that we find the most settings of Mass movements of the time. Although their musical structure is generally conservative and simple, we can also discover in them a trait which points to the future: there is a tendency to place the given liturgical melody, the cantus firmus, once again in the upper voice, as in the period prior to 1100, when parts of the Mass were also set polyphonically. This means that the liturgical melody is once again audible as a whole, that is, as a melody. The cantus firmus no longer has the purely constructive–ideal significance which we observed, for example, in the Machaut Mass. It is not simply the representative of dogma. In England it is once again present as a continuous flow of sound, as living language.

This was also encouraged by the fluent nature of the sonorities in English music, to which the preference for thirds, as we have seen, made an essential contribution. Now sixths were added, strengthening the tendency of the thirds towards forward progression. Third–sixth sonorities were often employed to achieve movement in a certain direction, a progression of sonorities which led from one center of sound to another. A musical phrase of this kind, which seems natural to us, becomes the vehicle of a textual phrase, which thus takes on the character of something natural and fluid: Ex. 17. These

Ex. 17

Et   in   ter - ra   pax ho-mi - ni - bus   bo - nae vo - lun - ta - tis.

third–sixth sonorities, typical of the fourteenth and early fifteenth centuries, bring about a mild tension, a mobility. The static sound of the fifth, which was still contained in the triad, is here completely lacking; it has been replaced by the sixth. The concluding formula in Ex. 18a was transformed by means of improvised ornamentation (b) to the cadence in Ex. 18c. But in the fourteenth century, particularly

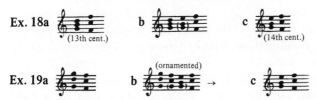

in England, third—sixth sonorities also originated directly out of the old fifth and fourth sonorities: Ex. 19. (These cadential formulae were further characterized by the so-called double leading-tone: *e-f* combined with *b-c*. This resulted in an accumulation of leading-tones, and accordingly of altered tones — see Ex. 17, *et in terra*).

The introduction of the third—sixth cadence formula is characteristic not only of England but of all polyphonic music of the fourteenth century. Only in England, however, was the third—sixth sonority made the basis of an entire technique. Only there is it put to consistent, clear and at the same time unadorned use in the manner of the example above. This practice is closely bound to the increasing prominence of the melodic factor, and also permits a straightforward psalmodic delivery of the text. In its pure form (progressions of third—sixth sonorities resolving into fifth—octave sonorities) it is called *fauxbourdon*.[12] It should be understood more as an aspect of tradition than as innovation: the adjacently positioned fourths which are formed between the upper voices are connected with the ancient practice of doubling and thus with the organum of the Carolingian era (see chapter 3 above); supporting the melody by means of adjacently placed sonorities of the same quality is related to reinforcement by fifths and octaves; similarly, the improvisational manner of performance which accompanies it is connected to the older practice of improvisation. All of this corresponds to the re-establishment of the tradition of placing the cantus firmus in the upper voice and to the resumption of polyphonic performance of Mass movements. Or should one go so far as to postulate a kind of subterranean survival of these practices in England from Carolingian times into the fourteenth century?

The musical setting of Mass movements flourishes in England particularly around the beginning of the fifteenth century. Here we also encounter for the first time a significant development in the setting of the Mass: an attempt is made to fuse the succession of individual movements of a Mass into a musical unity. This is achieved, for example, by centering all of the movements on the same melodic

motive or also by letting the upper voice begin melodically the same
way in all movements. By similar means melodic unity was also
encouraged within the individual movements. These developments in
the setting of the Mass are associated with the name of the great
English composer John Dunstable. As an example of the way in
which Dunstable was able to realize a natural flow of language
through free, prosodic rhythm and a melody based on psalmody, let
us look at the beginning of the upper voice of a three-voice Gloria.[13]

Ex. 20

Et   in   ter · · · ra____ pax homini-bus bo · nae   vo · lunta · tis.

The broad, tranquil flow of sound associates itself with a tendency
towards melodic–tonal unity: Ex. 20. We are already far removed
from the improvisatory ornamentation which was applied to the
sonorities of the twelfth century. But even when compared to
Machaut's tectonic building methods this formation of melody
appears forward-looking. And yet this music of Dunstable is rooted
in the conservative English practice of the fourteenth century.

Let us call to mind again the relationship between music and
liturgy in the fifteenth century. If one were to achieve a musical
unity of all of the Mass movements, it would not be possible to base
each individual movement on its relevant monophonic liturgical
melody as cantus firmus, since the melody is different for each
movement (Gloria, Credo, etc.). Now, however, that ideal association
with the sacred liturgical delivery of the text was no longer as
important as it had been earlier. The cantus firmus was no longer
regarded as a surrogate of the dogma. Its conceptual significance was
now narrowed down; it was looked upon as a purely musical phenomenon. The composer discovered in it that element which would
furnish the skeleton for the musical structure of a composition; it
appeared to be a useful means of achieving musical unity. Conse-
quently, one single cantus firmus was chosen for all movements of
the Mass; but while this produced *musical* unity in the Mass setting,
liturgical continuity was lost, for what was now employed as cantus
firmus was not the particular melody associated with the movement
in question, but rather any liturgical melody one pleased. Even in
this practice, then, we find a tendency which we have previously
encountered (p. 34). The musical setting of the Mass confronts us in

the fifteenth century not only as a component of the liturgy but also as an independent work of art.

Even during the first half of the fifteenth century Dunstable's music became widely known on the Continent. In this way there came about a union of the two musical currents, the English and the French, which led to a new development in the setting of the Mass. Paris was no longer the musical center of the Continent, as it had been in the fourteenth century; the focus had been shifted to Burgundian—Flemish—Dutch territory. Similarly, the now mannered, overly refined French style of composition was left behind. The first great master, Guillaume Dufay, who was active around the middle of the fifteenth century, absorbed the new traits of English music. He emphasized the melodic element. And yet we do not find in his music that naturalistically entwining, free melodic ornamentation of the English. His music is still determined to a considerable degree by the spirit of the French song, the chanson.

Its influence is felt even in the choice of a cantus firmus. In order to achieve musical unity in the Mass, a single cantus firmus was, as we have seen, taken as the basis of an entire Mass cycle and was then repeated in each of its sections. As a result this cantus firmus could no longer be the liturgical Gregorian melody of a particular Mass section. Now composers took yet a further step: since the cantus firmus no longer represented a concrete liturgical identity for the individual movement, the custom of drawing the cantus firmus from liturgical Gregorian chant was abandoned altogether. From now on it was thus possible to choose even a secular melody as cantus firmus. A secular chanson, for example a love song, could now provide the structural basis of the Mass. This cantus firmus was now usually placed in the tenor voice.

There followed two generations of composers of the so-called Netherlands school, with Ockeghem, Obrecht and Josquin Desprez, whose period of activity extended from the second half of the fifteenth century up to the beginning of the sixteenth. The earlier of these composers were concerned not so much with the setting of language as with the musical technique itself. The tradition-bound stance of the English, colored as it was by folk elements, was reinterpreted, when it was taken over on the Continent, in the light of the tradition which was there derived from the music of the fourteenth century; one returned, that is, to an absorption with tectonic structure in composition. With reference to the preceding chapter we could conclude: onto the English practice, which we must interpret

as the representation of the human being, is superimposed music as
independent ornament. Not until a century later was a synthesis
achieved by Palestrina and Lasso. The music of Dunstable, representing as it did the sum total and the creative renewal of the English
tradition, was more a challenge than a fulfillment; a challenge
directed towards the polyphonic musical realization of the Latin
language in its natural declamation. It was Palestrina who brought
about the fulfillment of this challenge in the realm of the Mass. This
was made possible, however, only through the musical—structural
efforts of the Netherlands composers.

Let us look for a moment at the change which took place in compositional technique. Flexibility in the use of sonorities had increased
immensely since the middle of the fifteenth century through the
establishment of four-voice writing. This favored the emergence of
sound progressions which formed an intrinsically consolidated unit.
The close affinity of the sonorities which stood in fourth- or fifth-
relationship to each other became apparent. Out of the cadential
formula described above in Exx. 18—19 there now emerged the formula shown in Ex. 21. The lower voice, which performs the step V—I,

Ex. 21

assumes from this time on a significance of its own.

For Ockeghem (see Ex. 37, p. 68) structural—musical problems
are in the foreground, music as "ornament." Specific figures, melodic
formulae combined in mosaic-like fashion, are frequently employed.
Various rhythmic groupings follow each other successively, are
meshed with or even layered on top of one another. Viewed as a
whole, the musical texture, and with it the delivery of the text, did
indeed achieve a fluidity reminiscent of Gregorian chant. A Mass by
Ockeghem, when compared, for example, with the Machaut Mass, is
felt to flow more smoothly, more evenly. The text, however, has not
yet been realized in its specific structure, in all its detail, with the
result that there remains an element of the accidental in the setting
of the individual syllables. And, accordingly, their underlay in manuscripts is frequently not pinpointed to individual notes. On those
occasions when the music does indeed mirror something of the
conceptual substance of the language, it does so by means of struc-

tural devices, thus employing, for example, a descending melodic line for the phrase *descendit de coelis*, or a rising motive to symbolize the raising of the cross at the *Crucifixus*.

For Obrecht, too, structural—musical problems remain in the foreground. He prefers to employ devices which are suggestive of instrumental methods of construction. Thus in one of his Sanctus settings the formula shown in Ex. 22 occurs eleven times consecu-

Ex. 22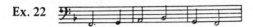

tively in the bass. Similarly, repetitions on successive pitch levels — so-called sequences — are often employed. In this way Obrecht achieves broad sound effects; that is, by using these methods he splits open the otherwise static sonorities and fills them out with apparent movement. That element which in the Middle Ages had been left to improvisation (see chapter 3 above) has here become part of the completed composition, part of the "res facta."

Josquin Desprez also makes use of devices similar to these. In his music, however, there is to be found another particular method of composition in its most mature form: so-called through-imitation. The technique of imitation, that is the successive entrance of voices with the same melodic motive, could be applied in a wide variety of ways: as structural basis for a section of the voice complex; conspicuously as melody; employing material from the cantus firmus; without cantus firmus; at different intervals (for example in unison, at the fifth, fourth, second). With Josquin it is *through-imitation* which predominates: within a particular movement each successive phrase of the text begins with a new point of imitation which is carried through all of the voices (compare Ex. 25, pp. 50f below).

The technique of through-imitation smoothed out the voice-leading and fused the voices with one another. In addition, however, it took on immense significance in the musical setting of the language: through repetition, in all voices, of the same beginning motive together with the words accompanying it, attention was drawn to the word as language, as an agent of sound, as linguistic-rhythmic structure. Points of imitation came into being, as it were, as word-engendered motives. The concept of the musical *theme* was thus first made possible through imitation. It is linked — and we must not overlook this sign of its birth — with the stamping of a linguistic pattern on our memory. Through-imitation no longer permitted multiple texting, since all of the voices were obliged to present the same text. (As late as 1451 Dufay was still composing motets with multiple texts!) This meant, however, a still further simplification in compositional technique: even though the single voices were treated individually, they exhibited the same substance — the same both musically and textually. Through-imitation further encouraged a musical subdivision corresponding to that of the text, since the individual sections always began with a new point of imitation. Finally, it is intimately connected with a momentous transformation of the musical fabric: the establishment of the *a cappella* mode of performance. Whereas up until that time the question of timbre had not been specifically determined by the composer (see p. 26), the performance of a musical work based on language was now thought of more and more as purely vocal. It seems natural to think of all the voices as being performed in the same (that is, the vocal) medium, since they are all sustained by the same textual and musical substance.

Both through-imitation and the *a cappella* ideal are essential characteristics of the music of Palestrina.

6 · Palestrina

With Palestrina (1525—94) the second phase of the musical setting of the Mass is completed (see p. 8), the phase which had begun with the Carolingian epoch. But Palestrina also represents the beginning of something new. He brought to fruition what had until that time been an open challenge and in this way steered the historical progress of music into new paths. In the present chapter we will concentrate our attention on these two questions: on Palestrina as conclusion and Palestrina as beginning. We will approach them from the following three points of view, with which we are already familiar: musical substance, relationship to language, status of the liturgy.

On Southern European ground there arose in the course of the first Christian millennium the monophonic Gregorian chant, which was intimately bound to the language and, accordingly, to the liturgy. On Northern, Germanic ground a starting point was provided in the Carolingian era by a self-contained music based on vertical sonorities, which existed independently of the liturgical language. Through its encounter with Christianity, i.e. with the Christian Word, the intrinsic significance of music was discovered, the sensuous nature of musical sonorities recognized. It was found that they could penetrate the language. There began a process of mutual influence, in which language became more musical and music took on aspects of language.

The initial consequence of this was – from the viewpoint of the language – a negative one. Language was taken over by music; it was split up by means of music, in that each of its syllables was weighted down with a sonority. The syntax of the whole was broken up into separate syllables. There was also a positive side to this, however: the individual syllable was now looked upon as an element, both musically as well as linguistically. The task now became to join the syllables with one another in a new way and thus to create linguistic syntax anew *out of the music* (see pp. 22f). This process was completed in stages, continuing over a period of seven centuries and only reaching its climax on Southern European ground in the music of Palestrina. Through the conceptual approach of the Italians the musical–structural technique of the North was pressed into the service of language as structure, as a linguistic form in which meaning is innately conveyed.

Let us call to mind once again the most important landmarks along this journey. First of all the metrical force of the language was realized musically. The syllables were regulated according to stricter or more flexible metric systems, as we ascertained, for example, in both of the complete Masses of the fourteenth century. The English, on the other hand, did not proceed, in the period around 1400 and thereafter, from a musical–constructive method of this kind but rather attempted to preserve the flow of the language with simple, straightforward musical techniques. But the internal factors in the music which are prerequisites for the accomplishment of this task had not yet reached maturity. In the following period the musical–constructive method was taken up once again on the continent. Composers who spread out from the Northeast of France to cover all of Europe reached a crucial confrontation with the materials of music.

Instead of proceeding with a musical–technical analysis at this point (in chapter 12 the reader will find further details of compositional methods from Palestrina to the composers of the Classic era), we will content ourselves with a more pictorial description. In the period prior to Palestrina music had not been reduced to its smallest components. It was rather like a tangle of simultaneously sounding tones, ornamental figures, rhythmic patterns. The musicians of the 120 years preceding Palestrina began to unravel the tangle. This process was brought to completion by Orlando di Lasso and Palestrina: the musical fabric was dissected into its fundamental components. Composers had gained control over the tone, had mastered it as a rhythmic, melodic and concordant element. Previously, single tones could not be separated out of the mass of sound (as, for example, in the ornamented sonorities of the early and high Middle Ages — see p. 25). Now it became possible to operate with the *single* tone; the composer could place it freely in the particular context of his choice. The musical material had for the first time been subordinated entirely to the human will. With that, however, there vanished that characteristic of earlier music which impressed us as *constructive*. From now on we have the feeling that the tones are joined together rhythmically, melodically and harmonically in a fully natural way. This arrangement is regarded as natural, however, because the human intellect — that is, the un-natural — has been able to take complete possession of the raw material. The human mind has forged an instrument for itself that allows the creation of an *intellectual* mirror of that which is commonly termed "natural."

From this vantage point the new relationship to language becomes understandable to us: music is now capable, using its own means, of mirroring the syntactic coherence of the language as a musical reality. Palestrina can relate the tones — order them, set them in motion — in such a way that the inherent progress of the music and that of the spoken sentence are in full correspondence with each other.

Two examples from Palestrina's Pope Marcellus Mass can serve to illustrate this: the *Et incarnatus* and the *Descendit*, both from the Credo.

The *Et incarnatus* (see Ex. 38, p. 69 below) consists of two statements which are linked to one another: *Et incarnatus est de Spiritu Sancto ex Maria Virgine* ("And was incarnate by the Holy Ghost of the Virgin Mary") and *et homo factus est* ("and was made man"). The phrases *Et incarnatus est* and *et homo factus est* are parallel to each other; there ensues a kind of linguistic rhyme. In the musical setting this is given expression:

Et in-car-na-tus est,   Et ho-mo fa-ctus est.

But there is also a difference: the phrase *Et incarnatus est* does not
by itself constitute a sentence but rather introduces the words *de
Spiritu Sancto ex Maria Virgine*, whereas *et homo factus est* constitutes a concluding statement that stands by itself. This, too, is
brought out in the music:

$$\text{o o o.} \quad \text{◻́ ◻́ ◻́}$$
$$\text{-natus est} \quad \text{fa-ctus est}$$

and the entire passage:

$$\text{◻ o o o o. ♩ o ♩♩ o o o. ♩ oo o o ◻}$$
Et in-car-na-tus est de Spi-ri-tu San-cto ex Ma-ri-a Vir-gi-ne
$$\text{◻ o o ◻ ◻ ◻}$$
Et ho-mo fa-ctus est.

As a second example let us examine the phrase which precedes
the one we have just discussed: *descendit de coelis* ("came down
from Heaven"): Ex. 23. This brief statement occurs twice in succession. This is not unnecessary repetition, however, for each time a

Ex. 23

different aspect is realized. The first time, the verb is made the focal

$$\text{♩ ◻ ♩ ♩ o ♩}$$

point; it is given the rhythm *descen-dit de coelis*. The other voices,
too, are characterized by a certain rhythmic activity, which is connected with the concept of the verb as active element. The second

time, on the other hand, it is the static character of the background image, the surrounding *de coelis*, which forms the focal point for the

o o o. ♩ ▭ ▭

rendering of the top voice. It is set to the rhythm *descendit de coe-lis*.

The way in which it is fitted out with sonorities also corresponds to this image: in the first statement of this text, that in which the idea of *descendit* predominates, the voices descend in stepwise motion, forming sonorities which are repeated a step lower each time. There results a *succession* of third—sixth sonorities, leading from a higher center of sound to a lower one (see p. 34). The second time, however, we hear a cadence-like progression which is localized around a single center of sound. This shows that, in the stage at which we find ourselves with Palestrina, language is captured in music as syntactic progression, as syntactic structure. This cannot, however, be separated from the realization of a certain aspect of the conceptual content as well. For that reason one should regard the descending movement of the sonorities not as a mere formality, but rather as a mode of dealing with the conceptual content of the language — a mode which is characteristic of the music of Palestrina.

From these brief examples we can infer the manner in which Palestrina's music comes to grips with language. What was inherent in the liturgically oriented music of the first thousand years has now been newly acquired by polyphonic music: once again it is a free gesture of speech, a linguistically logical and convincing sentence structure. The background to this event was provided by the historical confrontation — of the post-Carolingian era with the fact of early Christendom, of the North with the South, of music with language. In short, the background was provided by the intellectual—cultural maturation which took place from the Middle Ages to the Counter-Reformation.

For this transformation in the musical language corresponded to the change within the religious situation. The Reformation had drawn questions of religion into the center of awareness. The question of the liturgical function of music came to the fore. How it was resolved within the ambitus of the Reformation and the German language will concern us later. What happened there provided a new musical point of departure, a base for the emergence of the greatest German music, the music of Bach and the Viennese classical composers. In this chapter and the next, however, we will remain on Italian ground. It was here during the time of the Counter-

Reformation that the Council of Trent (1545–63) took place, which was also concerned with the question of liturgy and music. The Church demanded that music should respect the liturgical word. More important, however, than this all-too-frequently repeated observation is the fact that the culmination in the development of musical language achieved by Palestrina coincides with the culmination of the *liturgical* development of the Mass. In the era previous to this, around the fifteenth century, there existed a certain disorder with respect to the liturgy. It was not only the substance of the Mass that was misused – one thinks of Luther's accusations; its text, too, was corrupted. There arose local variations, superstitious additions or customs, and the like. At the time of the Council of Trent, therefore, the question of music was only one of many consequences of the liturgical re-formation of the Mass. For now the liturgical development of the Mass reached its culmination with the appearance of the definitive unified Missal, the Missal of Pope Pius V, around 1570. The erection of this powerful dike after fifteen centuries of growth and change coincides with the work of Palestrina.

Palestrina does not, however, represent only a conclusion. He became, as we have mentioned before, at the same time a beginning. With him music entered into a new phase. The human intellect had completely permeated the material of music; it had seized control over the single tone. Music could become the mirror of language, could embody the human being as a speaking entity. The synthesis between ornament (or construction) and human representation had taken place. Thus begins with Palestrina a new era in the history of music: music as the representation of man.

But the solution provided by Palestrina constitutes only one possibility. The inexhaustible ideal of language, and of man as a speaking creature, can be realized from various angles. How music since Palestrina has confronted it, what it has deemed essential in the word and in mankind at any given time, and which aspect it has been able to mirror: these are the questions which we must pursue from now on. As the example of the *descendit* from the Credo has already shown, Palestrina's music does indeed embody the language; at the same time, however, it mirrors it from one particular angle only. The sentence structure is here captured and the objective element of the conceptual content illuminated. Music appears here as a natural process. But the warmth, the inner fervor, the mystery of the incarnation have not yet become music, just as little as has the instant of the newly occurring, the unique, the historical event. These are aspects to be realized only in the music of later times, and they will therefore concern us in subsequent chapters (see particularly chapter 12, "Stages of musical reality").

7 · Monteverdi

Monteverdi (1567–1643) was not a composer of Masses in the sense that Palestrina was. His major field was secular music: opera and the madrigal. He did not write much church music. Of the three Masses which have been preserved, the Mass "In illo tempore" is the greatest.[14] He composed it in the year 1610 – that is, before he left Mantua and moved to Venice. It was written for Pope Paul V, a member of the Borghese family, who sought to enforce the ideals of the Counter-Reformation. With this work Monteverdi's towering personality created a musical interpretation of the Mass which cannot be ignored. Monteverdi constitutes a milestone in the growth of Western musical language. Through this setting of the Mass, as through his secular music, he contributed to the birth of the musical situation which in the following generation led to the assumption of leadership by German music. His Mass lays claim to a position of prominence not only within his own oeuvre. It is the only significant Mass of high quality which originated on Italian soil after Palestrina, the only one which is still closely bound to a specific ecclesiastical– liturgical outlook – a Mass of the Counter-Reformation, indeed perhaps *the* Mass of the Counter-Reformation. What later came into being on Germanic soil – works such as the great Masses of Bach and Beethoven – had, as we shall see later, a different musical heritage, a different significance. Between these two approaches lies the discovery of the German word through Luther and in music through Schütz.

We have already observed (pp. 36f) that it was possible to make use of a single cantus firmus in the composition of an entire Mass. However, as the word gradually began to be regarded musically once again as a vital, living element, composers were concerned that the declamation should be equally independent in each of the voices. Through-imitation (see pp. 39f) took on a decisive role. The musical fabric of Palestrina is based on this technique, and like all composers of his time Monteverdi, too, makes use of it, albeit not as consistently as Palestrina. The principle of continuous imitation was not, however, compatible with the rigid execution of a cantus firmus in long note values. In order to preserve the connection with a pre-existent music, a different technique was thus employed: instead of a monophonic cantus firmus one took as the basis of a Mass an entire polyphonic composition, for example a motet. The individual sections of each Mass movement began in the same way as the sections of the underlying composition, then continued independently. Masses of this kind (called "parody Masses") were also familiar to Palestrina's generation and earlier. Monteverdi's Mass is likewise based on a motet, namely the motet *In illo tempore* by the Netherlands composer Gombert, and thus bears the title "Missa In illo tempore." The fact that Monteverdi chose to base his Mass on the work of a Netherlands composer rather than on that of Palestrina, for example, is probably significant: Monteverdi, the great initiator, does not (strictly speaking) continue the work of Palestrina, the culminator. Indeed, what would there be which could be further developed? Monteverdi rather links up with that same earlier musical situation with which Palestrina had also been confronted. Thus we might say that from the same given circumstances he drew different conclusions from those of Palestrina.

In an earlier chapter we pointed out that music before Palestrina was essentially structurally conceived (see pp. 38f). This trait, this structural approach, is to be found again in Monteverdi. One frequently hears fixed melodic and rhythmic formulae which are repeated (on different pitch levels, for example) in a given voice. Such motives have a certain structural—instrumental character which is particularly evident in the bass. To that, however, is joined something new: the tendency to build a unity, a coherence in the progression of chords, a unifying principle which takes effect particularly at the cadence points, where all of the different elements are drawn together. We could also say that there is a tendency to subordinate the smaller units which are formed to a larger, all-embracing unit: Ex. 24 (p. 48). But the constructive technique also makes itself felt in the interpretation of the language. Let us look at the *Et incarnatus* from the Credo (see Ex. 39, p. 70 below), the same portion of text which served us as an example in the Mass of Palestrina. Monteverdi sets this section to the following rhythmic pattern:

𝄢 o. 𝅗𝅥o. 𝅗𝅥 o. 𝅗𝅥 o.𝅗𝅥o 𝄢 𝄢
Et in-carna-tus est de Spi-ritu San-cto

o. 𝅗𝅥oo o. 𝅗𝅥o. 𝅗𝅥 o. 𝅗𝅥 o. 𝅗𝅥 𝄢
ex Mari-a Vir-gine et ho-mo fac-tus est.

How straightforward, how human is the declamation of the same text in Palestrina (see Ex. 38, p. 69 below). This music, composed only a few decades before Monteverdi's Mass, removes us to a completely different world. We now seem to have left that natural, blossoming, unfettered linguistic gesture far behind.

In Monteverdi's music the text is not spoken as it was in Palestrina. The word is not convincing as a freely spoken word in the way in which it impressed us in Palestrina's Mass. Here it is rather hammered into our consciousness. One feels that the rigid, metrically forceful performance ideal of the Middle Ages is struggling to regain control.

Ex. 24   Monteverdi, Mass "In illo tempore"

And yet the Mass of Monteverdi cannot be considered only as backward-looking. The dogma which is, so to speak, hammered out is probably connected with the spirit of the Counter-Reformation and the wars of religion. But even leaving that aside, we should not look upon this interpretation of language as simply outmoded; it is not to be understood as the result of ineptitude. In it there vibrates something new, something which now fills the consciousness of the musician and takes on central importance. Here we catch a glimpse of the *significance* of the event to which the words refer. This is expressed, for example, in the rather subjective coloring, in the undertone tinged with emotion or even with pathos. It can also be felt, however, in the tendency to create unity. The sound of the moment is always subordinated to a higher unity. In this music there stirs a force which leads beyond the individual phrase. There emerges a dynamic tension, a craving for completion: the passage on *factus est* does not come to a close. Its final chord is open-ended; it requires something further as continuation, as conclusion. And so the *Et incarnatus est* is subordinated to a larger whole and is perceived, even in terms of compositional technique, as part of the entire Credo.

It is strange — but nonetheless instructive — that this new characteristic which is of such concern should be linked so intimately to the past, and in fact not to the recent past, to Palestrina, but rather to a period more remote in time.

From a liturgical point of view, however, this new approach to the word means a new freedom: the composer now strives more to realize the substantive content of the text, but this means at the same time realizing subjective expression. Music, which had grown in a constant confrontation with the word as the quintessential manifestation of the intellectual, had now reached a stage of sufficient maturity to permit its renewal through the German word.

8 · The German Language and Music

In order to understand how the German language was able to enrich music, it is necessary to contrast it with Latin. Although, as we have seen, textual content and meaning were not expressed in Gregorian chant, the Latin words were by no means rendered incomprehensible (see chapter 2). The coherence of the sentence, its logical assembly from various grammatical elements, its rhythmic articulation: all of these aspects are reflected in the music. The meaning conveyed by the language (for example, the content of *miserere nobis* or of *dona nobis pacem* — see p. 11) is not, however, realized musically.

The fact that the music obeys the gesture of the language, its structure, but does not embrace its meaning is not due to caprice, but rather points to a characteristic of the Latin language itself. In

Latin the act of speaking is not completely identical with the meaning. This peculiar circumstance is frequently overlooked. We have not made ourselves sufficiently aware of the fact that in languages such as ancient Greek, Latin and the Romance languages sound and meaning need not coincide. In ancient Greek this discrepancy was even more pronounced than in Latin, thanks to the decisive role played by quantitative metrics, and its consequences were of immense significance. This was noticed by Klopstock, who discovered the German language's inherent dependence on meaning and was as a result indignant — and rightly so — at what he felt to be the mechanical treatment of the language by the Greeks.

But Latin also distributes its accents according to principles other than meaning. Thus one and the same word can be accented differently according to the particular form in which it is presented. In the word *adorare*, for example, the accent can pass from one syllable to another: *adoráre* (to adore, to worship), but *adóro* (I adore); *adorátio* (adoration), but in the genitive case *adoratiónis*. Thus no single syllable when spoken is so wedded to the meaning, none bears so unequivocally the weight of presenting the meaning, that it should be inseparably joined to the accent. What is right for the language, however, is only fair for the music. Why should a musical setting take into consideration the content of meaning when even the *spoken* language does not do so? The language itself provides no encouragement in this direction. It distributes the accents not according to meaning but rather in order to clarify the sentence structure, to indicate the function of the word within the context of the sentence, to show, for instance, whether nominative or genitive case, singular or plural number, is intended. Gregorian chant is only being consistent when it follows similar principles in setting Latin texts to music and thus confines itself to clarifying the structure of the language. Similarly, it is understandable that Palestrina should lengthen the first syllable of the word *adorate* in Ex. 25, with no concern for the fact that it does not carry the accent.

The German language, however, behaves differently. Whereas in Latin the accent changes with the grammatical form (*adoráre*, *adóro*, *adorátio*, *adoratiónis*), German retains the same accentuation throughout all of the different forms: *veréhren*, *ich veréhre*, *veréhrte*, *wir veréhren*, *veréhrten*, *die Veréhrung*, *der Veréhrung*, etc. A wide gulf separates this linguistic attitude from that of Latin. For anyone making use of a language such as German, there opens up an essentially different aspect of reality. Here the spoken language coincides

Ex. 25

entirely with the meaning. The content of meaning not only is represented indirectly by means of the sentence structure, but is realized directly in the sound. Each word categorically demands that it sound only with that specific emphasis which is proper to it by virtue of the meaning. For here the accentuation (and the prolongation which accompanies it) is nothing other than the emphasis appropriate to the syllable which carries the meaning; and this syllable, of course, always remains the same with each basic word. This also brings about, however, the equivalence of word and emphasis, of language and expression, of objectification and self, of objectivity and subjectivity. The German language is attached to a human attitude in which the objective can only be viewed through the medium of the subjective, the outer world only through the inner. How great is the significance thus attached to accentuation, in that it becomes the vehicle of meaning, that it seems to take on the power of creating the word! And how fundamentally does this transform the task of music!

This is even more obvious if we consider that in a basic German word it is always the first syllable (which is often the only one) which carries the meaning and accordingly the accentuation: *Brót*, *Wásser*, *Hímmel*. Thus each German word, in its simple form, must begin with an accented syllable; it must be realized explosively, must be created each time out of nothing: *Váter*, *Tód*, *Lében*.[15] The unaccented prefixes are a different matter. They point to formation, to change, or to that which has been formed; they indicate a pulling-together, a summarization, and so on: for example, *verjúngt*, *gewórden*, *begreífen*, *herúnter*; and similarly: *und gíng*, *du blíckst*. If we transfer this to music, however, we obtain the two basic forms, the primary motives of modern musical–rhythmic organization: accented–unaccented (´ ˘) and unaccented–accented (˘ ´); for example, *Lébĕn*, *vĕrjúngt*. In music we call the first of these a downbeat, the second an upbeat. These two rhythmic elements receive a new position of honor: they are filled with meaning. Through them the musical fabric is newly formed; it takes on new significance.

A few examples may serve to illuminate the relationship between the linguistic and the musical viewpoint.

First, an example from a musical setting of language. In Schütz we find motives like: *dan-ket   und brachs* (from his St. Matthew Passion), to be performed: | ♪ ♪ 𝄾 ♪ | ♪ 𝄾 . This linguistically determined distribution of weight, this combination of downbeat and upbeat, becomes meaningful here; this rhythm is now binding. Indeed, rhythmic patterns of this kind speak so forcefully that they begin to lead an independent existence and in this way leave their mark on purely instrumental music.

Thus we may take the second example from instrumental music of a later period. A theme such as that of the Third *Leonora* Overture of Beethoven (Ex. 26) presupposes conceptual experiences of the kind which are expressed in the German language. Here downbeat and upbeat have specifically meaningful roles; they are filled with significance.

Ex. 26

But these same forces are also active in pure poetry which has not been set to music. Thus it is instructive to examine the application of crusis and anacrusis (downbeat and upbeat) particularly in the works of Hölderlin.[16] One could begin with simple combinations, such as:

Álter Vătér! Dŭ blíckst
(from *Das Ahnenbild*)

Or, to take an example from *Der Archipelagus*: following a description of the boldly aggressive merchant who likes to take risks, something completely different is to be touched upon, namely the youth caught up in his reflections. The powerful countermovement which thus becomes necessary is brought about by the interpolation, at a critical point, of the phrase *Ánders bewégt* ("differently moved"):

(. . . und öfters über des kühnen
Herkules Säulen hinaus, zu neuen seligen Inseln
Traven die Hoffnungen ihn und des Schiffes Flügel, indessen) –
Ánders bewégt – (am Gestade der Stadt ein einsamer Jüngling
Weilt und die Woge belauscht und Grosses ahndet der Ernste . . .)

Through this collision between downbeat and upbeat, which is determined by the meaning, and which, if correctly recited, cannot be disregarded, the significance of *anders bewegt* becomes like a solid body, capable of being grasped in our hands.

A further example (from *Die Entschlafenen*):

(. . . wo des göttlichen Geistes
Freude die Alternden all,) *álle die Tóten verjǘngt*

(. . . where the joy of the heavenly
Spirit the aging all, all the departed makes young).

After the downbeat pattern *alle die Toten* ("all the departed") there is a pause, and then abruptly, springing forth out of nowhere, the upbeat motive *verjüngt* (makes young), which overturns the downbeat rhythm, as if it were the spirit which works this miracle of rejuvenating the dead.

Let us, however, present a more extensive rhythmic combination (from the description of a raging battle at sea, in *Der Archipelagus*):

(Und entbrannter beginnt's; wie Paare ringender Männer,
Fassen die Schiffe sich an, in die Woge taumelt das Steuer,)
Úntĕr dĕn Stréitĕrn brícht dĕr Bódĕn, ŭnd Schíffĕr und Schíff sínkt.

The ground quakes, *not once* does the same metrical pattern return, the rhythm staggers between downbeat and upbeat, with each phrase another syllable breaks off, until even the final one "sinks."

′ ◡ ◡ ′ ◡	Unter den Streitern	('Neath the combatants
′ ◡ ′ ◡	bricht der Boden	splits the platform
◡ ′ ◡	und Schiffer	and shipmates
◡ ′	und Schiff	and ship
′	sinkt.	sink.)

In German, then, not only is the accentuation in itself dependent on the meaning, but beyond that even the rhythmic sentence structure, the rhythmic context, is determined by meaning. The sovereign freedom of man as a speaking being is discovered anew; a new vista opens up. The linguistic vessel of meaning dispenses completely with the ornamental and, by being subjugated to the meaning, is subsumed entirely under speech. Now the music which is born of this intellectual attitude can also realize more adequately its goal, the representation of man (see p. 28). Thus the Beethoven theme quoted above (Ex. 26) is not to be interpreted as a rhythmic motive in the sense of older music. The downbeat and the upbeat, which here collide with one another, are realities in the sphere of ideas, they partake somewhat of the importance of accentuation determined by meaning. On their own level they are incompatible; no transition is formed between them. They are held together as though by a transcendent power, and as a result they generate yet a third reality, effecting an integration of meaning.

Finally, let us refer to an example from the sphere of instrumental music, in which the connection to the German word has been confirmed by the composer himself. The final movement of Beethoven's last string quartet, op. 135 in F major, is built around the separate presentation and subsequent combination of two ideas, contrasted as

downbeat and upbeat: *Muss es sein?   Es muss sein!*

The place of honor which accentuation holds within the German language, as emphasis determined by meaning, combines with an absorbent energy developed by the accentuated root syllable. When one says *Himmel* or *Vater*, the first syllable of each word is not just accentuated more than the second, as for example in the Latin words *coelum* or *pater*. In the Latin the two syllables are placed next to one another, and the rhythmic gesture consists of two motions —

cóe - lúm — it is clearly divided. In the German words, on the other
  1   2

hand, the root syllable possesses such power that the second syllable is not simply placed next to it: it is subordinated to it. Here the rhythmic gesture consists of a single motion, an explosive attack, which receives a fading close: *Hímmel, Váter.* (The change in the duration of the syllables in the following example is also instructive:

Greek πᾰτήρ short–long, Latin *pătĕr* short–short, German *Váter* with meaning-determined extension of the root syllable and complete subordination of the final syllable.) This characteristic of the German language emphasizes even more strongly the central position of the stressed syllable. In music we encounter it again in the form of a new type of metrics. Just as in language, accentuation in music now also develops the same absorbent energy. The tone of greater weight rules over the others; it is placed above them in importance. In this way there arises a dynamic network of tension, a tendency to form units of ever-increasing importance — a process for which Monteverdi had paved the way on the musical side (see pp. 48f).

Since meaning and sound, meaning and speech now coincide completely with one another in the German language, the musical setting of language is also obliged to concern itself with meaning. Here music cannot be the mere vehicle of language as in Latin.

This applies in its strictest sense to the musical setting of prose. The song (Lied), on the other hand, provides a certain outlet. For here verses are being set to music. As a result the accentuation is already taken into account in the poetic meter. It is not absolutely necessary, however, to consider the meaning above and beyond that, since in a Lied we are considering an instance of music complete in itself. Thus if a religious congregation is to perform German liturgical texts, it is reasonable to employ Lieder. For the musical interpretation of German prose presupposes a personage who consciously comes to grips with the content of meaning in musical terms. Music of this kind, however, is not strictly liturgical music.

There remain, then, if the German language is to sound forth in the liturgy, only two possibilities: the sung Lied and spoken prose. These are also the only two forms which have been adopted in the German Lutheran Church. As a third possibility one could consider only the litany or rosary recitations common to the Catholic Church: the combined speaking of the congregation in alternating choirs, in the course of which a stationary column of sound comes into being of itself. Here there is no thought of meaning or even of the characteristics of a particular language. The chanting is imbedded in and surrounded by a unified flow of sound. But this type of musical setting of language lies, strictly speaking, outside of the historical confrontation between music and language.

The introduction of the German Lied into the church service was also encouraged by the historical situation. For the German language had, through the Lied, gained entrance into the liturgy even earlier, in the Middle Ages (see p. 14) — in the form, for example, of the

"Kyrioleise," the sacred folk songs which employed *Kyrioleis* (that is, *Kyrie eleison*) as a refrain — a phenomenon which reminds us of the trope. Or we could think, for example, of the sacred song *Christ ist erstanden*. That Luther, who discovered the German language anew, should also have introduced the German Lied was therefore well justified both practically and historically. The melodies could sometimes, to be sure, be derived from those of Gregorian chant, but they were transformed and appeared to have been born anew out of the spirit of the language. As an example let us take the German Sanctus from Luther's German Mass of 1526.[17] The German text is written in verse form. The melody is derived from a Gregorian Sanctus (XVII in the Editio Vaticana), which begins as in Ex. 27a.

The creative act which is evident in the German reshaping of this melody is admirable: Ex. 27b. Not only is the rhythmic configuration typical of the attitude of the German language, but also the melody exhibits that tendency towards unification, towards centralization, which is here expressed as the major mode.

Ex. 27a

San - - - ctus, San - - - ctus

b

Je - sai - a dem Propheten das geschah, daß   er im Geist den Herren sit-zen sah,

However, Luther appropriates the melody exactly when his models consist of verses which he translates. This is the case with hymns and sequences, of which the *Komm Gott Schöpfer* (the hymn *Veni creator*) will serve as an example.

The introduction of the German Lied does not, however, constitute a break with the liturgical tradition of the Mass. For verse — and not only in German but also in Latin — has never been the real liturgical language. Seen from a liturgical point of view it forms a secondary layer of language, introduced separately (see p. 14).

Luther's view of the relationship between the raw material of language and its musical setting is elucidated in the following two quotations: "On one occasion," Luther's biographer Mathesius tells us, he comes into the church at Eisenberg on Easter Sunday and is mightily angered that the Introit should be sung in German to the

Latin notes. When he later appears for dinner, the innkeeper asks him what is the matter. "I thought," says he, "that their ridiculous chant would make me sick. If we want to sing German, then let's sing good German songs; if we want to sing Latin, as schoolboys are supposed to do, then let's keep the old chant and its text . . . "[18]

And:

I would gladly have a German Mass today. I am also occupied with it. But I would very much like it to have a true German character. For to translate the Latin text and retain the Latin tone or notes has my sanction, though it doesn't sound polished or well done. Both the text and notes, the accent, melody, and manner of rendering must grow out of the true mother tongue and its inflection, otherwise all of it becomes an imitation, in the manner of the apes.[19]

But the German approach to language is also intimately bound up with the religious outlook of the Reformation. To a certain degree the abandonment of the Mass can be understood as a result of the introduction of the German language, quite apart from the theological ideas of the Reformation. Luther's discovery of the German language, his respect for the word in a special sense, and his disparagement of the Mass as action: all of these are closely connected with one another. The word as sound has for him nothing of the autonomously objective, nothing of the character of a formula (in the sense, for example, of a magic formula); it is not tangible as completed "work" — all of which is contained in the Latin word as a reflection of the attitude of antiquity. For Luther the word is nothing other than content of meaning here and now. "Here and now" and "content of meaning" actually refer to the same thing: the concept of the "here and now" negates the worship of the objectified word, of the word as hypostatized idea, as "form" which is present for its own sake, as an independent substance; but the concept of the word exclusively as content of meaning likewise implies the negation of that which has been objectified and that which can be likened to a formula. The here and now and the dependence on meaning are, however, the essential attributes of the German language. Because form and meaning coincide entirely — because the word as sonorous element has completely given up its independence and has been pressed into the service of meaning — the word takes on the character of the here and now as part of its very essence. It comes into being, as it were, only by virtue of sounding, out of nowhere, only to dissolve once again into nothing as the sound dies away. It has substance only as long as it is present as sound. (Compare also Luther's theological preference for the

"spoken word" as opposed to the lifeless "text" which is not consummated in our presence; and see the comments on language at the
beginning of this chapter.)

Thus we can say that the German language's dependence on
meaning and thereby its quality of immediate presence are forces on
which the Reformation also draws. Luther's creative act consists not
least in having subjected himself to the command of the German
word. He listened humbly to what the German language was trying
to tell him, and let it dictate its will to him.

This also characterizes Schütz. He alone fulfilled Luther's postulate that "text and notes, accent, melody and manner of rendering
must grow out of the true mother tongue and its inflection." In so
doing, however, he created — as was only logical — not a liturgical
but rather a personal form of musical setting.

9 · Schütz

We can understand that the attempts made during the sixteenth century to create a German liturgy of the traditional kind by adapting
the Latin Gregorian chant to German prose were not further pursued
at that time. When the Gregorian *Pater noster* melody (Ex. 28a) is
adapted, the linguistic gesture of the Latin *Pater noster / qui es in
coelis* is lost (Ex. 28b).[20] But in its details as well, the melody does

Ex. 28a
Pa‑ter no‑ster,qui es in coe‑lis:

b
Va‑ter un‑ser, der Du bist im Himmel,

not do the German language justice. Although the German words
Vater, *unser*, *Himmel* bear an external rhythmic correspondence to
their Latin counterparts *pater*, *noster*, *coelis*, they are in fact dis-
torted when the Gregorian method of performance is carried over.
For the Gregorian setting presupposes that the syllables are ranged in
succession as equals, whereas the German language categorically
demands subordination (see pp. 54f). The German *Vaterunser* (the

Lord's Prayer) is unfairly trivialized when set to the Latin melody; in particular, however, the setting of the word *Himmel* assumes an unbearably sentimental cast from the fact that the second syllable *-mel* is subordinated to the absorbent energy of *Him-*, resulting in an appoggiatura-like effect: Ex. 29a. This could be prevented only by singing the German word *Himmel* in the Latin manner, that is, by pronouncing it in an un-German way: Ex. 29b. Because of the root

Ex. 29a  b

emphasis of German, the direct juxtaposition of meaning-laden accentuations comes to the fore: *Ehe der Hähn krähen wird* (St. Matthew Passion). The musical setting derived from the Latin cannot do justice to this characteristic: Ex. 30.[21] The meaning-laden

Ex. 30a

Pri - us-quam gal - lus   can - tet

b

E - he der han kre-hen wirt

accentuation of a final syllable also becomes prominent, as here the syllable *wirt* in contrast to *cántĕt* (compare also, for example, *Zukomme uns dein Reich* with *ădvénĭat régnŭm túŭm*). These characteristics strengthen the synthetic–consolidating tendencies of the German, whereas the Latin appears analytic–juxtapositional in contrast. We are also reminded of the example of *adorate Dominum* (see pp. 50f above), which found an adequate musical setting in Palestrina's analytic–juxtapositional composition, where it flourishes as a radiant melody. In contrast, the German *verehrt den Herrn* or *bétet den Herrn án* exhibits an approach to language which demands an entirely different kind of musical setting from that of Palestrina.

The coincidence of meaning and sound creates the impression that the word comes into existence only through its enunciation (see also pp. 50f), that enunciation of the word and event are identical Thus the impression that something is happening forces itself upon us. When we read of Peter, in the Latin: *Et egressus foras* ("and he went forth," St. Matthew Passion), the action is described indirectly through the syntactic construction (which, to be sure, makes it perfectly intelligible). In German, however, the passage is formulated

und ging hinaus — and he has really departed! The notion of an
event forces itself upon us. Thus the formula-like setting of the Latin
(Ex. 31a) is unconvincing when applied to the German (Ex. 31b).
But in Schütz's setting (Ex. 31c) the music really speaks German. It
is not, however, a liturgical formula which can be applied at will, but
rather a unique act. For the musical setting of German prose is
intimately bound up with the creative act with its personal commitment to the meaning of the words.

When Luther in the German Mass and Walther in the chorale-
Passion attempted to adapt the Latin recitation and psalm tones to
the German language, they were frequently obliged to modify the
Latin formulae in the direction of accentuation determined by
meaning, though sometimes to a scarcely noticeable extent. The
setting of German prose to music, however, demanded a transformation in musical thinking down to its very roots. This musical setting
was created by Heinrich Schütz. That his music cannot be derived
from the musical trends of his time alone but rather represents a
confrontation with the language could also be demonstrated by
means of a comparison of Schütz's settings of the same text in Latin
and in German. (A comparison, for example, of *Paratum cor meum*
with *Mein Herz ist bereit* (*Symphoniae Sacrae* I and II) is informative.)
    Schütz also composed German versions of parts of the Mass
which taken together can be viewed as a unified Mass (they are contained in the *Zwölf Geistliche Gesänge*,[22] published in 1657). Let us
examine a few passages from the Confession of Faith. Before we do
this, however, we will find it useful to recall the Latin setting and its
German adaptation: Ex. 32a–b.[23] Next to these we can also place
the Walther version, Ex. 32c, which clearly bends the formula-like
chant in the direction of accentuation dependent on meaning. The
beginning of the setting by Schütz is shown in Ex. 33.
    It will serve our purpose better, however, to leave the melodic–
harmonic aspect out of consideration and concentrate instead on the

Ex. 32

Ex. 33

rhythm, since it is here that the characteristics shared with the language become more obvious. The beginning has the rhythm

Ich glaube an einen einigen Gott. The long sustained *Ich* functions as a rallying-point. And now the music flows:

> *glaube an einen einigen Gott.*

Not until the word *Gott* do we find another sustained tone. This sentence, then, stands at the beginning of the Creed like an inscription, held together by the juxtaposition of the words *Ich* and *Gott*. A similar juxtaposition in Latin is inconceivable simply by virtue of the fact that the personal pronoun *Ich* is lacking.

   In German we find in place of the Latin *in unum Deum* the words *an einen einigen Gott*. If Schütz had set this rhythmically as

einen einigen Gott the words *einen* and *einigen* would have been too similar to one another. Through the reversal of the rhythm, however,

the word *einigen* receives the necessary emphasis: *einigen*. At the same time the important break in rhythmic flow before *Gott* is achieved: *einigen Gott.* By means of this slight rhythmic differen-

tiation, then, it suddenly becomes possible to place emphases on

both *einigen* and *Gott.*

There follows *allmächtigen Va-ter.* The musical setting of the

word *allmächtigen* illustrates the absorbent energy of the meaning-

laden syllable *mäch-,* to which the next two syllables are subordi-

nated; and subsequently the long-sustained *Va-ter* is full of ardour,

devotion and warmth.

Continuing on:

Schöp-fer Him-mels und der Er-den,
al - les was sicht-bar und un-sicht-bar ist.

The emphasis is placed not on the word *Schöpfer* taken by itself,

but rather on the thought that God is the creator of the universe, of

heaven *and* of earth: *Schöpfer Himmels und der Erden.* The second

line brings a parallel, an intensification of the thought: God is the

creator of heaven and earth, yes, of all things visible and invisible, of

the universe in its totality. This parallelism of thought is expressed in

the adoption of the same rhythm for both lines:

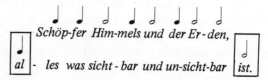

Schöp-fer Him-mels und der Er-den,
al - les was sicht-bar und un-sicht-bar ist.

The intensification, however, is expressed through the addition of

one tone at the beginning and one at the end of the second line.

Instead of *Schöpfer Him-* we have *alles was sicht-*, and instead of:

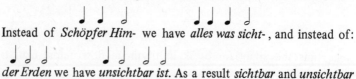

der Erden we have *unsichtbar ist.* As a result *sichtbar* and *unsichtbar* do not receive the same rhythm.

It is not *sichtbar und unsichtbar ist*

but rather *sichtbar und unsicht-* bar *ist.*

This is determined by the resemblance to *und der Erden*:

und der Er-den
und unsichtbar

This setting, however, also corresponds to the prose tendency: *sichtbar* and *unsichtbar* are not simply forced to adapt to one another in a mechanical way. The result is not the symmetrical sing-song rhythm

was sichtbar und unsichtbar ist.

We are compelled to grasp the meaning of the word *unsichtbar* separately:

was sichtbar und unsichtbar, ist.

The passage

welcher für uns Men - schen

und um un-ser Seligkeit wil - len

consists of two parallel components. The second component brings about an intensification of the preceding one, which is achieved by taking advantage of the absorbent energy of the root syllable *Se-*:

Seligkeit. We perceive the sermon-like attitude, the emphatic point-

ing out, the forceful and therefore affect-laden speech, the dynamic and ever-intensified manner of presentation. We do not find either the freely suspended sound of the word as part of the sentence, as in Palestrina, or its compelling force as dogma, as in Monteverdi. Instead, what rules here is the active, apostolic desire to convince. The corresponding passage from the Pope Marcellus Mass of Palestrina reads:

qui propter nos ho - mines

et propter nostram salu - tem

(To facilitate a comparison with Schütz the note values have been halved.) And with its melody this reads as in Ex. 34. The rhythm is

Ex. 34

Qui propter nos ho · · · · mi·nes et propter no·stram sa · · lu·tem

similar to the setting by Schütz. It would in fact be possible to adapt the German text to it:

welcher für uns Men - schen

und um un-ser Se-ligkeit willen

This external correspondence allows us to comprehend even more clearly the differences in the two approaches. With Palestrina the equalistic–analytic approach prevails; no emphasis, no intensification, no formation of a dynamic unity are to be found; no action, no emotion, no sermon-like tendencies are noticeable. This music wants nothing more than to enable the word to sound forth freely as a natural phenomenon.

In *vom Himmel kommen ist* the emphasis is placed (aside from that on *Himmel*) on the word *ist* rather than on *kommen*; as if Schütz wanted to strengthen the pronouncement, the actual event, what has been completed: *kommen ist*. And in comparison the analytic–detached word-placement of the Latin, the freely suspended

musical setting of Palestrina: *descendit de coe - lis* (see Ex. 23, p. 43 above).

As a final example let us compare the phrase

(von der) Jung - frauen Ma-ri - a

by Schütz (see Ex. 40, p. 71 below) with the corresponding

(ex) *Ma-ri-a Vir-gi-ne*

by Palestrina. In the German version two meaning-laden and therefore accentuated syllables are placed directly next to one another (see pp. 50ff): *Júng-fráu-*; then follow a downbeat pattern and an upbeat pattern: *-fráu-en* and *Ma-ri-(a)*. Here the caesura which results from the direct juxtaposition of downbeat and upbeat functions as a colon, a pause before pronouncement of the name – *Júngfráuen*: *María*. Palestrina's setting presents a situation which cannot be compared to this. The musical questions which arose in the setting by Schütz are here unknown. They make no sense, not so much because different compositional techniques are represented but rather because *Jungfrauen* and *virgine* are differently constituted linguistic realities. The human–intellectual viewpoints on which they rest are totally different.

We might add, that in the Palestrina the entire *Et incarnatus* passage is determined by the liturgical attitude of kneeling, whereas in the Schütz it is the unique personal interpretation of the word which is decisive.

In the Catholic Mass the sacramental words are spoken in a low voice by the priest during the Consecration. Thus they do not form part of the musical Mass; they are not set to music. Schütz, however, who composed for the Lutheran Church, included them in his *Zwölf Geistliche Gesänge*. The German language made this possible. He was able to give musical realization to the here and now, the meaning, but also to the introspection and warmth, the flowing quality.

A fundamental transformation had taken place within the span of a few decades. It cannot, however, be understood in the spirit of continuity in the strict sense. Music had not changed within the single category of the liturgical Latin Mass. For the seventeenth century was not a liturgical century. Its inclinations and the traditional liturgy were two separate worlds.[24] The liturgical–Catholic music of the Mass no longer formed the focal point of activity. The lesser masters who carried on the tradition of the liturgical Latin Mass are marginal figures. In the Protestant sphere, as well, there was no liturgical–musical Mass. But the center of the human–musical sphere of activity shifted, as a result of the breakthrough of the German word, from the liturgical Mass setting of the Latin to free

composition in the spirit of the German language. From Palestrina
by way of Monteverdi, it is now Schütz who takes the fate of Western music in his hand. The spark leaps across.

As an essential characteristic of Monteverdi's music we noted the
tendency towards the formation of a dynamic unity. Here can also
be found the reason why the music, for example, of Italy did not
continue on in a straight line. The spark leaps across to Germany
because this new musical attitude finds its innermost justification in
the German linguistic attitude. Monteverdi uncovered a side of music
which revealed its close affinity to the German word. Only through
the alliance with the German language did these beginnings lead to a
renewal of music, and to the emergence of the instrumental-musical
way of thinking which characterizes Bach and the Viennese classical
composers.

10 · Instrumental Music and J. S. Bach

From Gregorian chant to the music of Schütz, the musical realization of language was the main intention of composition. A particular aspect of the sounding language was singled out, determined
musically and placed in the foreground. With J.S. Bach this situation
changes: the main concern of music is not the language but rather
the meaning behind the language as perceived by the composer.
Since the time of Bach language has been only an agent; it is understood as a mere sign which points to something else. For musicians
up to and including Schütz, then, language as sound and composition
are identical; and since Bach this has changed. We will now concern
ourselves with this question.

Let us call to mind again the musical settings of the *Et incarnatus*.
Traditionally it was usual to perform this passage, which tells of the
incarnation of Christ, in a slow tempo, and in fact with everyone
kneeling. The attitude of reverence is also expressed in the simplicity
of the setting.

In the Gregorian version (see pp. 10ff) the individual grammatical
unit is expressed as a gesture of speech; the musical progression
sounds forth as living language: Ex. 35.

In the two Masses from the fourteenth century, the Mass of

Ex. 35

Et incar-natus est de Spi-ri-tu Sancto ex _ Ma-ri - a ,Vir-gi · ne: Et homo factus est.

Tournai and the Machaut Mass (see pp. 32f), the sentence is assembled from its individual syllables. Here the language has become rigid. It is spelled out emphatically: Ex. 36.[25]

Ex. 36   Machaut, Mass

With Ockeghem (see pp. 38f) the sentence is once again reproduced as a unit — now utilizing the new methods of polyphonic music. As far as the details are concerned, however, it is performed not as living language but rather following the medieval outlook: Ex. 37 (p. 68).[26]

In Palestrina's setting (see pp. 42f) the language is presented as living Latin not only when taken as a whole but also with relation to the single syllable. It is a natural manner of speaking, an unconfined and therefore convincing language: Ex. 38 (p. 69).

Monteverdi's setting (see pp. 47f) declaims the text with subjectively colored emphasis. It is imbued with the significance of the content of the language. Dynamic tension arises. There is a desire to form the individual unit as part of the whole: Ex. 39 (p. 70).

In the preceding chapter we observed how meaning and sound coincide in the German language. For this reason Schütz goes beyond Monteverdi and realizes the context of the language in music: Ex. 40 (p. 71).

What, however, is the case with Bach? Let us call to mind the setting of the *Et incarnatus* from his B minor Mass.

Ex. 37   Ockeghem, Mass "Fors seulement"

The musical realization of this passage from the Profession of Faith has represented a challenge to the musician ever since its inception in the fourth century. The series of interpretations which we have examined creates, evidently, something more than an accidental, arbitrarily composed mosaic. A certain logic rules; an inner relationship exists between each new setting and its predecessors. The power of memory is at work in a highly creative way. We don't wish to miss a single link. Only the sum total of the interpretations permits us to reach an awareness of the single purpose which lies behind and extends beyond them. We realize that Bach's setting, too, does not stand by itself but rather represents a continuation of the dialogue which has been going on since the earliest centuries of Christendom.

Ex. 38   Palestrina, Pope Marcellus Mass

The *Et incarnatus* of Bach is one of those compositions about which we like to say that in their earnestness, their depth of feeling, their creative flight they leave the words far behind and express the inexpressible. This conclusion, however, is not quite accurate. For to Bach music is not an interpretation of the sounding language, and thus it cannot transcend language. Bach pursues other goals. He no longer employs language as a resonant—perceptible form of meaning; he regards it not as an autonomous conceptual structure, as linguistic form, but rather as a sign for relationships of meaning which are not

Ex. 39 Monteverdi, Mass "In illo tempore"

of a specifically linguistic nature, as a mere reference to that which is meant. This permits him to realize his conception as purely musical meaning. He cannot therefore continue to pursue vocal music directly, since this had matured precisely as sounding language. And thus it is that Bach's music is intrinsically instrumental. The essentially new aspect of the B minor Mass compared with the music of Schütz and that of earlier settings is the instrumentalization of the music. Only this permits Bach to make tangible other relationships

Ex. 40   Schütz, *Zwölf Geistliche Gesänge*

of meaning than those which are contained within the spoken language. In the *Et incarnatus* he can thus realize the essential meaning of the sentence and its specific content by means of the instrumental motive which is woven around the passage (see Ex. 42, below). It is *this* which determines the musical event, *this* which sustains the vocal parts. But even in the latter there resides an instrumental substance. The descending steps (Ex. 41) which are responsible for the inexorable solemnity of the passage, this subdivision of the chord, cannot be considered an intrinsically vocal musical motive but has instead an instrumental character.

Ex. 41

However, the fact that instrumental music has become so important can be attributed to the phase which preceded it. As we have observed in chapter 3, the historical origin of polyphony in the Carolingian era was a result of the confrontation of the Christian word with a sonorous—instrumental conception of music. Out of this there developed a music which was closely tied to language but which exhibited an essentially sonorous–instrumental structure. This contradiction had, however, to be resolved. There thus began a process of mutual interpenetration between these heterogeneous approaches to music. In our earlier discussion (see p. 40) we singled out two separate possibilities: music as ornament and music as the representation of man. At the base of the former is to be found the sonorous–instrumental conception; at that of the latter, music as the realization of language. When, therefore, music as the representation of man, and thus the infusion of music with language on the one hand and of language with music on the other, was singled out as the goal of Western music, this meant in a stricter sense the infusion of the *instrumental* element with language and the *instrumentalization* of the language. This process continued for several centuries. At first this juxtaposition of the two components found expression in the fact that voices and instruments could be freely employed and intermixed during performance. The strict separation between vocal and instrumental, as we know it today, did not exist at that time. Not until the sixteenth century was the complete infusion of music with language achieved. This was mirrored in the strict use of voices alone (cf. p. 40) in the *a cappella* ideal of the music of Palestrina.

But only at this point did the origin of an independent instrumental music as the opposite pole become possible. Not that instrumental music had never existed before; but it had constituted a lower species, the music of minstrels. However, now that music had become completely infused with language, it was possible to develop an instrumental way of thinking as well. This was not only expressed in the rise of the instrumental art music of the seventeenth century (with which we will not concern ourselves here): perhaps even more impressive was the new alliance between the language-bound and the instrumental-musical ways of thinking, which now joined forces as vocal music with instrumental accompaniment. Only independent partners can become allies. They had gained this independence, however, only in the sixteenth century. Only the stage of *a cappella* performance made possible the new phase, into which language-infused music could now enter.

It is peculiar that this new phase, song with instrumental accompaniment, did not constitute a compromise or a setback in the pursuit of the goal of music as the representation of man, but that instead it realized this ideal in a certain sense more clearly than *a cappella* music itself. For now the instrumental part took over the specifically musical–structural role, thus freeing the vocal part to serve other functions. There emerged the *stile recitativo*, the foundation of Monteverdi's opera. Here the vocal part was analytic–connective; it mirrored the linguistic element, the flowing word. The instrumental part was constructive–syntactic and took over the establishment of musical relationships of meaning (one such instrumental–structural agent, for example, is the *basso ostinato*, a bass formula repeated many times over, which is combined with an ever-changing upper part — see Ex. 22, p. 39 above — and other variation techniques belong in this context as well). The free rendering of the text, unencumbered by the musical construction, is supported structurally by the instrumental accompaniment.

It appears that a similar situation may also have been reflected in the term *concerto*, which came into use shortly before 1600 (in the works of Andrea and Giovanni Gabrieli, Viadana, et al.) — that is, the combination of the vocal–melodic with the instrumental–structural element. In the designation *concerti spirituali* or *geistliche Konzerte* (works for voice with instrumental accompaniment) as used, for example, by Schütz, the original meaning of the term *concerto* is still present. This was then combined with the notion of cooperation and competition between solo voices and instruments or among different instruments, as well as between groups of instruments or between solo and tutti.

In the case of both the *stile recitativo* and the *concerto*, however, the larger structural concept is that of the *thorough-bass*: the structural foundation is provided by the bass, which forms the skeleton of the harmonic progression and is performed instrumentally. The bass part proceeds continuously. Only the bass line is notated: the harmonic progression, the chords, are improvised by the performer, generally on a keyboard instrument (organ or harpsichord), following the directions (the so-called figures) with which the bass part is usually provided (see also pp. 104–7 below).

The vocal — or, later, also instrumental — complex of upper parts can now devote itself, unencumbered by structural considerations, to an interpretation of the word, to the melodic element; it can serve as an agent of expression. There were also, to be sure, compositions in which this clear distinction between the melodic and the structural, between vocal and instrumental parts, was not carried through: in the works of Monteverdi and Schütz, for example, which we discussed in previous chapters. But the new spirit can be felt even in these. Thus particularly the bass part in Monteverdi's Mass (see

Exx. 24 and 39, pp. 48 and 70), which can in fact, if desired, also be performed as an instrumental basso continuo, exhibits a tectonic–instrumental structure, even though the Mass still belongs formally to the tradition of Palestrina, of *a cappella* polyphony. The Passions composed by Schütz, which for liturgical reasons are to be performed without instrumental accompaniment, represent a purely linguistic–musical, expressive type of musical setting, in which the concept of a supporting harmonic foundation, albeit invisible, as it were, is also contained. In Schütz's unadorned polyphonic mass settings in *a cappella* style (see pp. 60f), the separation in function between the complex of upper voices and the bass is evident in spite of the expressive treatment of the text.

Thus the thorough-bass complex, the instrumental accompaniment, had nothing to do with the presentation of the language as sound; it was not directly responsible for the interpretation of the language. Nothing was more likely than that this element of composition, which was independent of the word, should have been newly pressed into service in the realization of meaning. This instrumental manner of thinking could no longer, however, see as its foremost task the presentation of language as sound. It followed instead its own paths, for it was not able to link up directly with the language. Here, then, we find a starting point from which we can understand such a phenomenon as the instrumental fabric of the *Et incarnatus* in Bach's B minor Mass (see pp. 66f and 69f). The instrumental element – which in the beginning formed an integral part of Western polyphony but had then been excluded as an explicit factor through the ever-increasing importance of the vocal element, a process culminating with Palestrina – now slips in through an unnoticed door. It now even claims the right to the instrumentalization no longer of the language but, rather, directly of the context of meaning; it claims the right to become an independent agent of meaning. Nor was this claim illegitimate. For Western polyphony had been born under the sign of the instrumental element, and following a history of almost a thousand years, it had now reached maturity.

And yet this history had been enacted as the constant confrontation with the word. It was thus thanks to this past history, to its earlier lack of independence, that instrumental music was now able to become an independent agent of meaning. Only this realization provides us with a basis for attaining a deeper understanding of the transformation before which we now stand. The instrumental fabric of Bach's *Et incarnatus* – the figure in Ex. 42, for example – appears

Ex. 42

to "speak" to us. This is characteristic of all of the greatest instrumental music, of the music of Bach and the Viennese classical masters. Where does it come from? The answer to this question provides us with an essential insight to the instrumental music of that time. It has already been implied above (see p. 52): musical motives, musical rhythms, which had originated in the setting of language became vividly and indelibly imprinted on the human mind, so that they began to lead a life of their own and as a result to impregnate instrumental music as well. The musical figures which had been created by Monteverdi, and especially by Schütz in settings of the German word, were experienced so intensely — were so graphic, so sculptured, so strongly stamped on the memory — that they could now, saturated as they were with meaning, also be employed without the word. With Schütz the history of music as the realization of sounding language came to an end. If we examine Western music from the viewpoint of its relationship to language, this constitutes the most decisive turning point of its history.

From now on music articulates as if it were speaking — to be precise, as if it were speaking German. It has in common with the German language the dynamic quality, the tendency to form successively higher units, and in addition the cultural—intellectual outlook, the unpretentious contemplative quality, the appeal determined as it were by meaning. Its distribution of stresses has the dignity of accentuation determined by meaning. Thus Schütz does not represent only a conclusion. With him begins the great period of what could in a deeper sense be called German music. Schütz, Bach, the Viennese classical masters (including Schubert): these three successive phenomena, comparable in their intensity to volcanic eruptions, are based on the cultural—intellectual outlook which animates the German language. Let us remind ourselves that the independent stance of music would not have been possible had not composers previously set German — that is, language as the context of meaning — to music, had not the works of Schütz existed. For the connecting link between the formal setting of language to music and its employment as a mere symbol of content is in fact language sounding forth as meaning. The German language, however, which determined the music of the immediately preceding stage, is in this respect the furthest advanced of the European languages.

With the transfer to the purely instrumental level, however, new conclusions were drawn: instrumental music rationalizes and systematizes; only in this process does it come into its own. In Schütz's settings of German prose we do not yet find, for example, the musical measure carried through as a principle. And yet it was in connection with the setting of the German language that we saw those elements of the later measure which determine meaning, the downbeat and the upbeat — in fact, metrics (see pp. 52 and 55) — take on a new significance. There these features were still in fermentation. Only as a result of thinking in instrumental terms were these conclusions gradually reached.

The newly emerging music is not, however, based solely on its immediately preceding phase. Instrumentalization allows composition to include all of the earlier stages of Western music within itself. Let us illustrate this by means of an instrumental work by Bach which could not have existed without its relationship to language: a chorale prelude.

A chorale prelude is an organ piece which is based on the melody of a given chorale. It is, then, a purely instrumental piece which, however, is related to an originally sung melody, to a sung text, a chorale. The first strophe of the chorale *Vor Deinen Thron* ("Before thy throne") reads as follows:

> Vor Deinen Thron tret ich hiermit,
> O Gott, und Dich demütlich bitt:
> Wend Dein genädig Angesicht
> Von mir betrübtem Sünder nicht.

The melody consists likewise of four lines, and the sections of Bach's chorale prelude correspond to them. The piece is written in four parts. The three lower parts begin successively with the initial line of melody in short note values. Only after the three lower parts have entered is the melody presented in long note values in the upper part, as it would be if sung, while the three lower voices are further elaborated.[27] Successive sections are constructed in a like manner, and the only additional feature is the continued treatment of melodic material from previous lines in the three lower voices while the new melodic line is being presented in the upper voice each time. This means, however, that in spirit the different lines are being presented simultaneously with regard to the text as well, so that the content of the chorale confronts us in concentrated form — a process which is incompatible with natural speech.

As we have already implied, the historical dimension approaches us in Bach's music as something now present. The various historical phases of the encounter of musical sonority with the word are here reflected, as for example the reference to the Faith, the visible religious connection through the chorale. This reminds us of the oldest stage of polyphony in Western history, in which we were confronted with liturgical chant as the representative of dogma (see chapter 3). In Bach's music the chorale melody is taken over in its ecclesiastically artless, folklike form as a symbol of the religious idea, as quotation, and is employed as the structural foundation for an autonomous piece of instrumental polyphony. And yet at the same time we become aware of two differences. In the first place, the sonority, the "polyphony" of that early-medieval period was still an amorphous mass; its parts had not yet been consciously worked out. Because of that it could not yet do justice to the full content of the word. Here, however, with Bach, it is the product of a thoroughly mature polyphonic art. Secondly, with Bach it is not the early-medieval Latin chant, the representative of a transcendental idea, which is present but rather the new folklike German chorale, both as language and as melody, and sustained by the human warmth of the individual. However, this leads not to a bridging-over but rather to an intensification of the contrast between the given chorale and its polyphonic treatment: this simple, intimate and folklike melody is meant to be perceptible to the senses as a whole. It sounds forth as a naive folk song, while at the same time we are aware of a structure thoroughly permeated by the human intellect, in the polyphony of the three lower parts. This rests in the lap of the chorale and is surrounded by it. But as a result the true activity of the intellect stands out all the more strongly against the background of the folklike—religious quality; the confrontation, indeed the coercive joining together, of the primary substance and the polyphonic structure becomes all the more significant.

Let us direct our attention to this polyphonic structure: here, in the events taking place in the three lower parts, is reflected the path which had been traversed since the early-medieval treatment of the chant melody. We can illustrate this by means of a few examples. When, at the end of the piece, following what had been up until then a never-slackening web of polyphonic activity, the last line (next-to-last measure) resounds once again like an echo thrown back from the furthest wall of the church, but this time as a summarizing gesture by the lower parts moving together, it is like a reminiscence from another world. One is reminded of that medieval time, in which the word was still comprehended and declaimed in music solely as a sonorous—metrical entity, as something seen from the outside, an object.

The simultaneous sounding of the different lines of the chorale, and thus the simultaneous performance of the different lines of text in the listener's mind, is reminiscent, on the other hand, of the high Middle Ages (see pp. 29f). This process, although contrary to the laws of language, is thoroughly justified, as long as the word is comprehended musically only as the representative of an idea which is paraphrased and as sonorous—metrical material. Just as the different texts were held together by a common idea, so the different parts of the music are joined by the common harmonic foundation.

The thematic structure and the inner articulation correspond to a more mature phase of the musical interpretation of the word; the three lower parts carry excerpts from the chorale melody, but they articulate them in short note values. It is as if one were constantly declaiming the words mentally. The individual lines of the chorale melody are transformed into themes which present the text accordingly. Here is reflected the phase which vocal music reached in the fifteenth and sixteenth centuries: the language is here comprehended musically as a naturally declaimed sentence. At the same time the presentation of the word is still governed by a quality which is cool, crystal clear, unapproachable. This is the situation when, for example, in the sixteenth century the word *descendit* in the Credo is illustrated by descending scalelike passages (see pp. 38f and 43f), or when in Bach the text passage *betrübten Sünder* ("distressed sinner") takes on — in the form of a darkening achieved by numerous cutting dissonances — a pitilessly cold and piercing character, becoming as it were the portrait of the fraudulent and sinful.

When, finally, in the melodic elaboration of the individual lines are expressed the subjective experience, the intimate warmth of the personality, the representation, with blood coursing through its veins, and the breath of the living subject, the very personal and sweetly cajoling petition, the affect of pain — all of this reminds us of the vocal music of Monteverdi and Schütz.

As for Bach, we are now speaking of a purely instrumental piece. Independent instrumental music, including chorale preludes, had, to be sure, existed in the sixteenth and seventeenth centuries. But purely instrumental art music was at that time still in its beginnings; it still betrayed its origins in the common everyday instrumental music of the handworker, the minstrel; it still bore clearly the marks of the mere impulse to play on an instrument. Bach was the first to infuse instrumental music completely with the spirit of rationality, by enriching it with the sum total of the historical accumulation of meaning which had taken place in the sphere of vocal music. He experienced the musical language of the instrumental sphere so intensely and was so possessed by the desire to "speak" forcibly through music that he was able to imprint the characteristics of linguistic forcefulness upon his material.

Thus Bach's strict polyphony, which distinguishes him from his contemporaries, must be viewed not as a conservative trait but rather as the result of its connection with that form of polyphonic music which was bound to language. To become conscious of the breadth of Bach's musical span we need only to call to mind the two cornerstones of his creative work: on the one hand polyphony, on the other his adherence to the chorale as an idea provided from the outside, a reflection back to the origins of Western music.

Nor does this apply solely to the chorale prelude. In a broader sense it is also applicable to other forms of instrumental music; to the fugue, for example, which, we should note, bears very clearly the stamp of its origins in the vocal music of the sixteenth century. Preludes and similar instrumental pieces (for example, those which precede fugues) have the character of preparation, as if staking out the territory. The real intensification takes place, however, only with the fugue, that representative of vocal music. Here, in the fugue, the theme is similar to a chorale melody in its representation of an idea. The instrumental themes have been made vocal, or, better expressed, they have taken on a structure similar to that of language. And conversely, vocal music receives an instrumental type of inner organization; it is infused with instrumental motives and thus interpreted as instrumental music. In Bach the minstrel, the organist, the cantor, and the court Kapellmeister are all united in one person. One could say that since instrumental music has become independent, the inner reason for a division of music into vocal and instrumental categories has ceased to exist. Vocal music can be reproduced properly only when it is performed as if it were instrumental — that is, on the basis of its purely instrumental motivic organization. And instrumental music should be performed as if it were vocal — that is, as if it were speaking, with the forcefulness of speech.

The musical composition has thus become so laden with meaning that it can stand in lieu of language in its ordinary sense. It combines restraint with fervor, objectivity with complete involvement of the subject, the craft of the handworker with the ultimate assumption of responsibility by the individual.

Let us examine further examples from the B minor Mass. The speaking quality of the new instrumental manner of composing now permitted vocal passages to be introduced instrumentally, since the two methods of expression had been adapted to one another. The theme of the Kyrie, for example, is first presented instrumentally and has in fact an instrumental character. How eloquent this theme really is becomes apparent, however, when it is presented vocally:

Ex. 43

Ky - ri - e   e - le .   .   .   . i - son, Ky - ri - e - le -

Rendering the musical composition independent of a textual prototype allows the music to capture components of meaning which are not directly represented in the sounding language. At the very beginning of the Mass, the invocation *Kyrie* by the entire choir plus the instruments expresses something different from what could ever be contained in a spoken pronouncement of the text *Kyrie eleison*. The idea that the Mass is hereby begun, this idea of a beseeching opening gesture, has here become music.

Similarly, the radiant beginning of the Gloria in D major in 3/8 time, with the sound of trumpets and drums, cannot be understood merely as a rendition of the text *Gloria in excelsis Deo* ("Glory be to God on high"). It introduces the entire Gloria and points to the liturgical attitude which has become traditional for this part of the Mass.

Its counterpart is formed by the conclusion of the Gloria in 3/4 time, at *cum Sancto Spiritu in gloria Dei Patris. Amen* ("With the Holy Spirit in the glory of God the Father. Amen"). Who could venture to describe in words the creative power of imagination which is at work here? It is not the language which is meant to be expressed here. Bach allows himself to be inspired by the content in order to create an independent work of music, which belongs — it is safe to say — among the greatest monuments of the art which have come down to us.

In the Sanctus the frequently repeated rhythmic figure

Sanctus Dominus Deus Sabaoth.

is introduced in the bass shortly after the beginning. The instrumental manner in which it is employed illustrates the new function of language within composition.

The employment of language by the now-independent instrumental music as a mere indication of intended meaning is connected, as we have seen (see p. 75), with the attitude of the German language. It is also this emancipation of music from language that now permits composers to set once again the traditional Latin text which had been handed down through the centuries. For now their composition need not be based strictly on the language which it employs. Thus the music can also elucidate relationships of meaning, even when this contradicts the structure of the Latin language. To put it in a somewhat simplified and exaggerated form, it is now possible to translate a Latin (or even an Italian) text directly into German music, to represent it as German intellectual substance. And, conversely, from now on all music of the Western world was able — so far as this is possible at all — to speak German, as it were, by taking over elements of the German musical structure of composition.

It is a further consequence of the autonomous stance of music that Bach divides each Mass section into individual movements (some of them for soloists as well), for example *Et incarnatus*, *Crucifixus*, *Et resurrexit*. By means of this division Bach interprets the text in his own way. This also allows him, moreover, to confer on each part of the text which has been thus subdivided its own basic musical character. Symbols or metaphors, which are represented by musical means, can also determine the content of the individual movements. Thus the symbolism of numbers frequently serves as a point of departure.

On the basis of the chorale prelude *Vor Deinen Thron* we pointed out the significance of cantus-firmus treatment within the instrumental way of thinking. The employment of two different melodies as cantus firmus is also encountered. In the Kyrie in F major, for example, Bach combines the melody *Christe, Du Lamm Gottes* ("Christ, thou Lamb of God") with the *Kyrie eleison* melody which follows the phrase *O Du Gottes Lamm, das der Welt Sünde trägt* ("O thou Lamb of God that bears the sins of the world") in the litany. The two cantus firmi are connected by the idea (Lamb of God) common to both. Only the *Kyrie* text is sung, however.

The vocal execution of a cantus firmus can, however, result in the simultaneous singing of two different texts. If the cantus firmus is derived from a Gregorian melody, we are even provided with a concrete reminiscence of the music of the past. As an example of the latter let us look at the beginning of the Credo of the B minor Mass. Bach employs the intonation *Credo in unum Deum* (see Ex. 2, p. 11 above) as cantus firmus, partly vocally and partly instrumentally. It does not, however, sound forth as a living phrase of language as in Gregorian chant, but has rather become rigid as in the polyphony of the Middle Ages, falling apart into separate syllables. Only the accentuation is taken into account, as metric scansion, similar to medieval practice:

Ex. 44

Cre - do in u - num De - um

What we have just said gives rise to a general observation: since music is following its own paths, it often needs to take nothing more of the language into consideration than its accentuation. This reminds us of the Middle Ages, which set language to music mainly from the viewpoint of the metric stress.

We know little about the origin of the B minor Mass. Bach dedicated the Kyrie and Gloria in 1733 to his sovereign, August II, Elector of Saxony. The remaining movements were composed in the years following.

The electoral court was Catholic. Was the B minor Mass, then, written for the Catholic service? It is understandable that Bach should have offered his sovereign a work which could be accommodated to the Catholic–Latin rites. We cannot conclude from this, however, that the work was conceived as Catholic liturgical music. For one thing, Latin Mass movements, particularly the Kyrie and Gloria, were still employed at that time within the Protestant tradition. It has been pointed out, however, and justifiably so, that the B minor Mass cannot be looked upon as liturgical music of any kind, whether Catholic or Protestant.

The spiritual roots and the spiritual breadth of this work may perhaps become more apparent if we remind ourselves of the situation that obtained at that time in the history of the liturgy of the Mass and in the change within the language of music.

We have already observed (chapter 6) that the liturgical formation of the Mass culminated in the final standardized Missal around 1570. This also transformed, however, the significance of the musical setting of the Mass. The Catholic liturgy remained the same thereafter; music, however, continued to change. Whereas music up until that time formed a part of liturgical history, it now of necessity became isolated, for the liturgy, removing itself from the process of change, thrust music from its side (see also pp. 65f). Thus the musical setting of the Mass since the seventeenth century belongs no longer to the history of the liturgy but rather solely to the history of music. In addition the history of the liturgy now ceases to affect the vital center of the Christian–spiritual sphere. Newly composed liturgical music therefore gradually sank down to a level of secondary significance. Conversely, a work such as the B minor Mass could only remain on the outside of the contemporary liturgical scene.

But at the same time the transformation in the language of music brought about an essential change — one could even say a cultural–intellectual upheaval. We have seen that music now became instrumentalized. We can express the same idea, however, by saying that the musical–rational process was now secularized, in that it merged with the instrumental craft of the minstrel. Or can it perhaps be better expressed: the general sphere of the cultural–intellectual was now joined to the Christian; it was inundated by the Christian sphere. Now there is no longer a single category of music, so-called sacred music, which is the responsible representative of Christianity; rather, music as a whole has assimilated the Christian element. Just as a new unity had now been created from vocal and instrumental music, there also emerged out of the earlier categories of sacred music and secular music a single art newly born in the spirit of Christianity. In the Middle Ages human rationality was present more in the form of different categories. With Bach, however, a new era is born, which sees the mark of this rationality increasingly in its unity. The human spirit has taken a further step in capturing the whole of reality. A further fusion of the secular craft of the minstrel with religious solemnity has taken place. It represents not a dilution of the art of music but rather its intensification.

11 · The Viennese Classical Masters

The Viennese classical masters, Haydn, Mozart and Beethoven, think, as did Bach, in instrumental terms. Thus the observation made at the end of the previous chapter regarding the combination of the sacred sphere with the secular applies also to them. They, too, employ language as a mere indication of the intended meaning, which is then captured through instrumental techniques. Nevertheless, in the music of the Viennese classical composers both the form and the gesture of the language are given direct expression. This takes place, however, in a special sense, and in a new way. If we attempt to translate the new aspect of Viennese classical music into more general cultural—intellectual terms, we can describe it as the realization of action, of specifically human action. And precisely this quality can be visualized as the acquiring of a new musical relationship to the word. At this point, however, it will be useful to proceed from secular music.

Let us first examine a pre-classical work. Out of the new relationship to the theater, to the represented and thus also to the speaking person, had emerged a new kind of music. In Pergolesi's comic opera *La serva padrona* (1733) the music is not so much concerned with mirroring an affect or even a change of affect. What the composer sets to music is the situation, the action, the events on the stage, the incidents taking place before our eyes, in our presence, here and now. Our attention is drawn through the music to the interpreter as the person taking action, as the *actor*. Through the music we participate in his actions, as in the first aria sung by Uberto: Ex. 45. The affect behind this speech — the humor, let us say, of a peevish, irritated old man — is not the primary content of the music here.

Ex. 45   *La serva padrona*, no. 1

84

Pergolesi does not understand the words from the viewpoint of the stationary affect but rather from that of the action, that is to say, as if the words were testifying to events taking place here and now, before our eyes, in our presence. To look upon reality in this way, however, means to visualize it as something discontinuous and thus also unpredictable. For the situation changes abruptly from one moment to the next, unforeseen from the outside. It arises each time out of the interaction between person and event, out of the unexpectedly emerging and until then nonexistent occurrence. It is in this sense that the verbal content is here understood: (1) *aspettáre*: one waits, for a long period, anxiously; (2) *e non venire*: suddenly, abruptly, a new situation materializes, through recognition of the fact that the expected arrival does not take place.

What Pergolesi, responding to the dictates of the moment, was more or less compelled to impose on the music is now realized by the young Mozart through means intrinsic to music: Ex. 46. *A forza di martelli, di martelli, mart-è-lli — il ferro si riduce.* "Under the force of the hammer, the hammer, the h-a-mmer" — and now

Ex. 46   *La finta giardiniera*, no. 5

suddenly, abruptly, a new situation materializes — "the iron gives way." The analogy to *aspettare – e non venire* is unmistakable. In both cases, from stereotyped, proverb-like phrases the moment of the event is singled out, and from that an important action, an active musical reality, is created. In both cases there is a situation of intensified waiting, of perseverance, and its sequel, precipitated by a sudden change in the external circumstances (here by the sudden yielding of the iron).

An example from the early works of Haydn may serve to illuminate more closely the technical musical side of the conceptual standpoint: Ex. 47. The decisive gap is provided by the eighth-rest at the end of measure 16, preceding the beginning of the pattern in measures 17–20. In the first sixteen measures the initial impulse of the upbeat predominates: ♪│ ♩ . Through omission of the upbeat prior to measure 17 there occurs a break, a gap; one stumbles: a break in continuity achieved quite deliberately. In this way the moment of the here and now is captured in the compositional technique of the music. There now follows, in measures 17–20, a motive beginning with a downbeat: │ ♫♫♫ ♩ ↑ │. With the end of measure 20, however, the upbeat motive asserts itself once again. It enters,

Ex. 47 String Quartet op. 1 no. 1, 1st movement

willfully and determinedly, on the sixth eighth-note of this measure (again, discontinuity). But the downbeat pattern of measures 17—20 has caused confusion. The upbeat motive, the main theme of the piece, cannot regain control quite immediately. The phrasing

♪|♪♫♫♪|♫♪♪ 7 demonstrates how unsteady it is at

first. Only in the final two measures does it seem convincing:

♪|♪ 7 ♪♫♪|♩ 7 ⸰ ‖.

Initially, then, the upbeat motive is presented simply in the manner of a declaration. Only when it is treated appropriately does it assume for us the nature of an event.

A second important characteristic of the construction can also be observed. Until measure 22 the concluding chord, which represents a release of tension, falls each time on the weak part of the measure, whereas the dominant (or subdominant) chord, representing the main point of tension, coincides with its strong part (measures 4, 8, 9–14, 17–20, 22). Up until this point the piece proceeds according to the formula |V–I| instead of the usual V|I — that is, with a continual conflict between the measure and the harmonic structure. (This harmonic pattern does, however, correspond to the rhythmic form of the main theme, which ends on the weak part of the

measure: ♪|♩ ♪♩ ♪|♩ ♪♩. Only in the last two measures of

the example is the conflict resolved, in that the harmonic progression |V–I| is counteracted by the energetic impulse that enters freely in measure 23. Only at this point does the tonic chord form a true conclusion.

The harmonic symbol V–I, then, was not at one with the unit of the measure. Harmonic symbol and metric distribution of weight did not form an inseparable unit, but were rather treated individually.

The reversal of the original rhythmic pattern is also related to this: instead of the earlier uniform feminine ending (as at NB in the last rhythmic example above), the ending is now masculine:

We saw, however, that the conflict between the upbeat and downbeat motives also continued up until just these final two measures, and that a resolution was achieved only with these same two final measures. This give-and-take between the two motives, then, was also connected with the metric instability of the harmonic basis. The separate, independent treatment of the measure unit on the one hand and of its filling-in with notes on the other has been presented to us from various angles. After Haydn has roused us in this way, awakening our awareness of this innovation, he now shows us in the final two measures — but only here — what unification is capable of accomplishing.

Let us summarize:

In the passage which we have just examined, the compositional technique rests on the separate treatment of the metric distribution of weight and the filling-in with notes. Two structural methods are employed: (a) the alternation between presence and absence of the eighth-note upbeat, and (b) the alternation in the arrangement of the measure: │ ♩. ♩. │ and ♩. │ ♩. . However, these methods are not applied within the various themes as well. The first one begins consistently with an upbeat (measures 1–8, and similarly 9–16), the second one consistently with a downbeat (measures 17–20); the ending returns to the upbeat. This, however, presents the decisive counterbalanced reversal │ ♩. ♩. │ →♩. │ ♩. . Nor are the two methods combined with one another: the pattern without the upbeat (measures 17–20) is not, for instance, also joined with the measure arrangement ♩. │ ♩. . Thus the individual themes still have something of the pre-classic inflexibility. They lack the suppleness and pliancy which they would later acquire. In place of this, external means were applied, such as contrasts in dynamics and in instrumentation (see measures 1–4).

This was only a beginning. Where it was to lead can be seen in an example from the works of the mature Haydn: Ex. 48. Here there are none of the abrupt contrasts found in the first quartet. The melody appears to form a uniform, continuous line. It is thoroughly pliable; we detect an air of unusual clarity. This stems from the fact that the melody only appears to be continuous. In reality the methods which we have observed above are now present (differently than in the first quartet) within this *single* theme and are in fact

Ex. 48   String Quartet op. 33 no. 2, last movement

coupled with one another. The theme, in 6/8 time as in the first quartet, begins, like it, with an upbeat ♪ | ♩ ; the first and second sections close, as there, on the weak part of the measure (measures 2 and 4) | ♫♩ ♪ ♩ . But measures 5–7 bring about a transformation: they close on the first beat of measure 7; the subsequent cadence (in measures 7–8) summarizes the movement of the entire passage by using a metric pattern which reverses that pattern of the preceding half-cadences (measures 2 and 4) – ♫♩ | ♩ – that is, the measure arrangement is ♩. | ♩. instead of | ♩. ♩. . At the same time, moreover, it presents as a new motive a pattern beginning without an upbeat: 7 ♫♩ | ♩ instead of, for instance, ♪ ♫♩ | ♩. This pattern, its discontinuity, is in fact underlined and given emphasis by the appoggiatura ♪♩ . Here, then, we find that the cadence of measures 1–8 is counterbalanced in a double sense. (Also instructive is the comparison with a theme such as that of the third movement of Bach's Fifth "Brandenburg" Concerto, with its continuous, uniform forward movement.)

That a compositional structure of this kind should form the basis of a musical setting of the word as action is obvious. Without it Mozart's musical theater is inconceivable. The finales of his operas provide excellent examples. In them a further concentration is achieved: not only are the above-mentioned methods applied within a single small section, but in addition each of the parts (vocal and also instrumental) makes its own use of them so that different figures can enter simultaneously and interact with one another.[28]

We can see that the music of the Viennese classical composers, like that of Bach, allows no distinction between vocal and instrumental compositional techniques which can be justified from within. An intrinsically instrumental approach is the prerequisite to vocal music as well. Only the *recitative* behaves differently, in particular, the secco recitative accompanied in a simple chordal style. In comparison to the succession of formally structured musical numbers the recitative appears to be a differently conceived, unfamiliar category, whether it be encountered in an Italian opera by Mozart or in a Bach Passion. For this reason doubt has even been cast upon the so-called aesthetic unity of the Mozart opera, and the recitative has been termed a hybrid product between language and music. From the vantage point which we have now reached, however, it is indeed possible to understand the recitative. Let us remember that only since the process of the instrumentalization of music set in has it emerged as a category sharply distinct from the formally enclosed musical numbers which surround it; only since that time has it been perceived as a foreign body to be tolerated, accepted along with the rest. (The *stile recitativo* of Monteverdi — see p. 73 — is not to be equated with secco recitative. It formed the basis of the composition; out of it, arioso, aria or duet emerged imperceptibly in the course of the piece.) It is the recitative which now represents the opposite pole from the instrumentalized form of musical composition, since the contrast between the language-bound and instrumental viewpoints (see p. 73) was no longer expressed in any other way. The language had, to be sure, assumed the function of a symbol within this new music (see pp. 69f), but as *linguistic* form it found a place of refuge in the recitative. The *stile recitativo* had formed the basis of the new phase of composition for Monteverdi and Schütz. Out of that affect-laden musical speech had emerged not only vocal categories such as the arioso and the aria: it was also the source of the speaking quality which characterizes the new instrumentalized form of composition. Now the *stile recitativo*, having enriched music to an extraordinary extent, sank to the level of a mere schematic allusion to the body of language as sound — it took on, that is, the form of the newer recitative. The recitative serves as a reminder of the original function of music from Gregorian chant through Schütz: of the musical realization of language as a body of sound.

Let us turn our attention again to the musical setting of the Mass.

The two older masters of the Viennese classical period, Haydn and Mozart, composed numerous Mass settings; but the third, Beethoven, wrote only two Masses. All of them are, with one exception, Masses composed for use in the liturgy, notwithstanding the fact that some of their movements come up to the level of the great Viennese classical masterpieces. The only exception is Beethoven's second Mass, his Missa Solemnis, composed in the years 1818–23. Even this work was originally intended for a church service, namely for the investiture of the Archduke Rudolf as Archbishop of Olmütz (the work is also dedicated to him). But it did not come into common liturgical use. Beethoven himself referred to the Missa Solemnis as his greatest and most fully developed work. It was first performed in concert on 24 March 1824 in St. Petersburg at the request of Prince Galitzin. Beethoven himself never heard a complete performance of the work. Only parts of it were presented in a concert in Vienna in May 1824.

But before we concern ourselves with the Missa Solemnis, let us look at an example from the liturgical Masses of the Viennese classical period: at Joseph Haydn's so-called "Nelson" Mass, composed in 1798. The title refers to the traditional claim that the Benedictus in particular was written under the impact of Nelson's victory at the naval battle of Abukir. Haydn's setting of the Benedictus includes fanfares and forceful outbursts of a kind which were otherwise not customary in this part of the Mass. The text reads *Benedictus qui venit in nomine Domini* ("Blessed is he who comes in the Name of the Lord"). It forms the second part of the Sanctus and is sung, in the Catholic service, after the Consecration. In listening to this movement we are struck in particular by two features. First, it does not, even though it is part of a liturgical composition, appear to fulfill a liturgical function. And secondly, the text is here declaimed again from the viewpoint of speaking, again – we might say – in a natural way and not, for example, as in Bach's B minor Mass. These two points are interrelated. The Mass is, in fact, intended for liturgical use, but for liturgical use by the people of that time; it presupposes the congregation of that time. This in turn is the prerequisite for the easily understandable, straightforward and natural declamation of the text which we have observed. It is also known that the reigning emperor of the 1780s, the enlightened Joseph II himself, exerted great influence in this respect. The secularized society borne on the ideas of the Enlightenment sought even in the church service the pleasant, festive atmosphere of a Sunday, an air of joyful entertainment. It also looked for these qualities in music, which is not to say that the individual worshipper was not capable on occasion of devoting himself with true piety to the central liturgical event. The words "Blessed is he who comes in the Name of the Lord" do not in themselves preclude a musical interpretation such as Haydn's — and society, without feeling itself hampered by the connection with the liturgy, found pleasure in the brilliant inspiration. Haydn, however, could allow himself such freedom only because he was completely immersed in liturgical tradition, because he felt himself secure within it. The Mass as liturgy is for him self-evident. He had, after all, begun as a choirboy in the cathedral of St. Stephen in Vienna. He captures precisely the attitude which the churchgoer expects from each movement and the atmosphere which is to be conveyed: thus, for example, in the *Dona nobis pacem* from the Agnus Dei there is the typical atmosphere of the closing of the Mass, the communion of souls, the "Ite missa est," the dismissal, the contentment, the backward glance. In this manner, however, Haydn achieves something which we had not yet encountered in earlier music: he creates an effect of conclusion which pertains to the Mass as a whole; he makes the musical Mass a closed unit.

As might be expected, Mass settings of this kind do not as a rule strive for a profound interpretation of the meaning of the text. Thus the passage *Et incarnatus* from the "Nelson" Mass offers no essential contribution to an interpretation of the mystery of the incarnation. One notices instead the straightforward, folklike quality of the piece, its affinity to folk song.

If we wish to discover what the great master Haydn is capable of expressing musically, we must look beyond his Masses to those works in which he has bequeathed us something valid for all ages: to the instrumental works and the late oratorios.

But let us turn now to Beethoven's Missa Solemnis. The most obvious course of action would be to single out the *Et incarnatus* and to relate it to the succession of musical settings of this passage which we have already come to know. But this would not be appropriate here, for it is not reasonable to extract this passage from the whole of the Missa Solemnis.

Before looking at it one must have assimilated the preceding *descendit de coelis* ("came down from Heaven"); and the *descendit*, for its part, can be understood musically only as part of the Credo, just as the musical succession of movements from the Kyrie to the Agnus bears within itself the stamp of necessity. So forceful is the closed nature of the Missa Solemnis; such is the unity of this work. In order to illuminate Beethoven's *Et incarnatus* properly, it would be necessary to examine in depth the entire preceding part of the Mass. Here, however, we must content ourselves with a few comments.

When listening to the Missa Solemnis, one has the feeling that everything preceding the *Et incarnatus* is in the nature of a preparation. So novel is the reality which touches us at the incarnation, so fervent is the *Et homo factus est* ("And was made man"), embedded in the center of the entire Mass.

The Kyrie constitutes the opening. The very first chord brings about a concentration unknown in music prior to Beethoven. Whereas in Bach's B minor Mass only the four introductory measures represent the suppliant opening gesture, here the Kyrie *as a whole* assumes the nature of an introduction. One finds not only the suppliant quality of the gesture. In this Kyrie is captured the trait of welding together, of collecting, of consecrating, which characterizes the cry of the litany, *Kyrie eleison*. The Kyrie originated as a cry of entreaty within the litany. In chapter 2 we quoted a description from the sixth century: the hordes from seven Roman basilicas which wandered praying through the city, crying *Kyrie eleison* in the streets, until they were joined in a single litany before the main church. It is as if this memorable moment had been re-enacted in Beethoven and at the same time raised to universal significance.

The instrumentalization of the musical language which we observed in Bach is, of course, also present here. It is, however, joined to the easily understandable, speechlike declamation of the text as we found it in Haydn. Beethoven's manner of composition has the effect of being simpler than Bach's but in reality it is not; he represents a new stage, in which he is able to evoke an impression of simplicity. This signifies a synthesis of all that has gone before. This music interprets meaning as instrumental musical language; at the same time it realizes the language as sound in the sense of music prior to Bach.

Like the Kyrie the Gloria can be comprehended only as a whole. The outward sign of this is the fact that the conclusion reverts back to the beginning. Not until the sounding of the final chord do we grasp the unity of the movement. It begins with an Allegro vivace in 3/4 time.

There follows the middle section *Qui tollis*. Let us take an example from this section in order to point out the new relationship of Viennese classical music to the textual content. The text *miserere nobis* ("have mercy upon us") is presented by Beethoven several times in succession, declaimed differently each time. We have the impression that people standing across from us are just now, in our presence, speaking these words and giving them each time new significance. The continuity of speech, as it was present in music prior to the Viennese classical masters, appears here to have been transformed into a constant new emergence of speech. The individual, in speaking, seems to discover his own reality. It is as if he performed an action. Let us consider, for example, the sudden, unexpected jolt which separates two settings of the words *miserere nobis* from one another (Gloria, measures 291–2).

The continuity of speech appears here to have been turned into its opposite, into a discontinuity. In reality, however, the unity lies no longer on the level of the materially given but rather on that of the purely spiritual–intellectual; it lies in the unity of the comprehending intellect.

The third section of the Gloria, *in gloria Dei patris, Amen* is introduced by the phrase *Quoniam tu solus sanctus* ("For Thou only art holy"). This section concludes with the reappearance of the beginning of the Gloria, now as *Presto*. It forms a counterpart, equal in nobility, to Bach's setting (see p. 80).

The liturgical event was illuminated from two angles in the Kyrie and Gloria: as the procession of the congregation to the holy place, and as a Dionysian hymn of the angels, an echo from the chancel. There follows the Profession of Faith. Here the act of speaking takes on the nature of immediate presence. The first, frequently encountered word, *Credo*, is repeated several times: *Credo, credo.*

But here repetition adds to the meaning. The ruling idea here is that the words originate in our presence, that the speaker thereby discovers his own reality. This singular kind of action is already present in the first three introductory measures. Faith as a solid rock is not represented in an objective way: it is embraced by the individual in an act of free will.

It is understandable that, approached in this way, the incarnation must form the heart of the Mass. It opens the way to a glimpse of the secret of faith. The *Et incarnatus* is introduced by the words

Qui propter. Even the first phrase, *Qui propter nos homines et propter nostram salutem* ("Who for us men and for our salvation"), sheds a warmth unknown until this point. Its sources are the fervour and solemnity of the moment. The powerful second phrase, *descendit de coelis*, which almost forces its way into our presence with no warning, acting once again as something immediately present, originating unexpectedly before our very eyes, flings open the curtain. We hear the words of the incarnation, at first only the phrase *et incarnatus est de Spiritu Sancto ex Maria Virgine*. Whereas Bach immediately adjoins the words *et homo factus est*, still within the same movement, Beethoven separates them from the *Et incarnatus* in his setting. Comprehending language as action, he must distinguish rigorously between those words which describe the divine mystery of God-made-man on the one hand, *Et incarnatus est de Spiritu Sancto ex Maria Virgine*, and those which express the unique temporal–historical event on the other, *et homo factus est*.

How tangible have become here both the contrast and the unity which bind together human reality and the mystery which surrounds it!

Once the act of speaking and with it reality have been understood as something now present, taking place at this moment, and once the essential characteristic of mankind is seen in man as an active being, there can be no return to earlier stages. But forward progress is equally inconceivable. What, then, did the future bring?

12 · Stages of Musical Reality

With the last remark we pointed to the deep cleft which appears after the Viennese classical composers. If we wish, however, to understand better its origin and its significance, it will be necessary to inquire into the meaning of the events of music history up until this time. In the course of our presentation we have paid only slight attention to the technical musical foundations of composition since the time of Palestrina. Valid insight into the cultural–intellectual stance of this period can only be won, however, on the basis of a careful analysis of compositional method. Only contemplation of the ultimate prerequisites behind the material repository of meaning will permit us to penetrate to the real core of the matter, to that point from which intellectual conviction emerges as tangible compositional technique, as meaning converted into substance.

Let us examine musical composition from the time of Palestrina up to the Viennese classical composers. We will begin with Palestrina, since only at that stage does the human intellect succeed in penetrating completely the materials of music. We have already touched upon this aspect in chapter 6 (see pp. 42 and 45). Control had been achieved over the musical tone as a rhythmic, melodic and harmonic element. Palestrina is able to work with the individual tone.

We will attempt to clarify this. Western polyphony originated out of the confrontation between monophonic liturgical chant and a music founded on vertical sonorities. This resulted after the first millennium in the isolation of the individual sonorities. They separated themselves from the homogeneous body of sound and became independent (see pp. 24f). We observed, however, that the individual sonority of that time could not be identified with the chord of music after about 1600. The sonority encompasses within itself a movement, an oscillation of its components. This expressed itself in the improvisational practice of ornamentation. Let us proceed from the premise that we can more readily understand the emergence of polyphony up to the time of Palestrina if we take into consideration the transformation from improvisational practices to notationally fixed working-out of the details of a composition. This is not the least of the determinants out of which developed the art of melodic manipulation and of polyphonic intertwining of melodic lines. From the stage of improvisational ornamentation of individual sonorities stems the rule that only consonances may occur at accented metrical points. Consonances, however, are the components of the sonority, which is heard as a unified whole. Thus the rule states that these sonorities, which in fact determine the distribution of weight, must fall on the main points of rhythmic stress. What sounds between these points is not specified rationally, is not stated in the form of rules. Even though it may be set down in written form, it still belongs to the level of improvisation in a wider sense; it does not yet build an independent linear movement but represents the sonority itself, which is unfolding in time and, together with its ornamental figures, still constitutes a knot of sound which cannot be unraveled. The single tone cannot yet be isolated, cannot be separated out of the tangle of ornamentation. Those sonorities which emerge out of the ornamental figures between the main sonorities or pillars of sound are thus the product of chance. One cannot examine their formation in any detail, nor accept them at face value. The emergence of polyphony from the Middle Ages to Palestrina is characterized by the progressive clarification of voice-leading. The irrational figures ornamenting the sonority were gradually transformed into a web of rationally directed voices. However, this was made possible only through the dissection of the individual line into its component parts. Through isolation of the tone one became free to determine and justify its rhythmic, melodic and harmonic placement. The above-mentioned rule of placing a consonance at points of rhythmic stress retains its basic validity. But this forms the foundation of a new compositional technique which completely determines the voice-leading in all its details and the resulting consonances. This is not yet the case in the music of the Netherlands composers. Only in the music of Palestrina are the last elements of chance eliminated. For this reason his music also glides along more smoothly than that of the earlier composers. It employs fewer dissonances, less striking melodic and rhythmic motives. It would be incorrect, however, to characterize this as timorous and the dissonances of music before Palestrina as bold. The smoothness of Palestrina's composition is to be identified with the attainment of the level of strictly regulated polyphony.[29]

The melodic line is now put together from individual tones — it is com-posed in the strict sense of the word. There results an extremely supple and hence unobtrusive melodic line which appears to be completely natural, one which avoids any kind of sudden interruption and can be compared to "softly flowing water" (Jeppesen). Out of the complex of its compositional traits let us select but a few (any work of Palestrina's can be used as an example, in this case see those cited above on pages 43, 51 and 69). The notes proceed mainly in stepwise motion; as a rule, skips are filled in immediately thereafter; skips are avoided following an accented quarter-note (see Ex. 25, p. 51 above). A rising movement tends to slacken in motion, a falling one to accelerate. In Palestrina's melodic line there is no mere ornament or figuration; the individual tone is substantive. Thus there also appear no stereotyped formulae or sequences (that is, repetitions of a motive at different pitch levels), for anything of a formulaic nature would negate the independence of the individual tone.

In the determination of consonances the individual tone also forms the point of departure. In Palestrina's polyphony the voices must be allowed to proceed if possible without mutual interference.

For that reason the sonorities which are formed must be unobtrusive and are thus usually consonant. In other words, each individual tone is treated independently; its relationship to all that is sounding at the same time is examined. The tone as component of the melodic progression affirms the individual sonority resulting from the melodic progression and thus becomes its rational component. In this way, however, it ceases to be the result of chance, something uncontrolled as it were, with regard to the harmony as well.

To the earlier basic rule that accented main sonorities must be consonant there are now added various specific criteria which regulate the harmonies formed by the voices between the main consonances as well. Consonant sonorities form the foundation: the triad in root position (e.g. *d'-f'-a'*, as in m. 5 of Ex. 25) or in first inversion (e.g. *f'-a'-d''* in m. 2 of the same example). These can occur at any point. Dissonances, however, may be formed only under specific circumstances: they may occur only on unaccented beats and must in addition be introduced and resolved in stepwise motion. These are the so-called passing dissonances (e.g. in the tenor at m. 5 of Ex. 38, p. 69).

In addition to the foregoing there is another purposely dissonant formation: the suspension. It originates on the accented beat through postponement of the entrance of the expected consonance (e.g. Ex. 38, m. 5/6 in the alto). The suspension was first made possible through the strict separation of the treatment of consonance from that of dissonance. It also presupposes the systematic division of time through regular alternation between light and heavy impulses at half-note intervals $\left(\text{♩} \quad \text{♩} \right)$.[30] The suspension brings about a mild blockage which is resolved by the ensuing chord, as represented schematically in Ex. 49. Passing dissonances can be illustrated as in

Ex. 49

Ex. 50. The graphic indication beneath the staves in Exx. 49 and 50 is meant to show that the individual tone is treated as an independent element. In the passing dissonance, the consonant sonority is heard on the accented beat. On the unaccented beat this relationship

Ex. 50

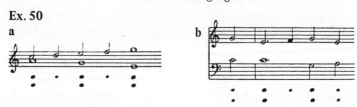

is dissolved, but the tone is justified in a linear sense as a passing tone; it leads stepwise to another consonance. Thus each tone is completely regulated both in its relationship to the simultaneously sounding tones and in the way in which it is introduced and followed. It is meant to be heard individually. Only this dissection carried through to the ultimate component, the individual tone, now permits a new kind of synthetic listening to emerge. Only now is it possible to comprehend the relationship which is illustrated above

(Ex. 49) in the schematic presentation of the suspension:

The consonant sonorities, the triad and its first inversion, are likewise meant to be heard individually. They are not subordinated to any higher unity. The triads frequently succeed one another in a progression (cf. p. 38) based upon the relationship represented by leaps of a fourth or fifth in the bass voice (see the progression of triads on G, C, F, C, G minor in the opening bars of Ex. 38). There results a back-and-forth movement between these sonorities, but they do not lose their independence. They do not form a dynamic whole; there are no tensions; rather, they are static. Thus they can also be placed next to each other in a manner which appears to us abrupt and unexpected (see m. 6–7 of Ex. 38, the triads on A and F). The third–sixth (first-inversion) sonorities either appear between them or build series – parallel progressions as in the fourteenth or fifteenth century (see pp. 34f, and compare the *descendit* of Palestrina, m. 1f of Ex. 23). Just as with the tones of the melody, then, there emerges in the treatment of the sonorities, too, an impression of unregulated co-existence. The arrangement of both tones and sonorities has – we could say – a merely introspective character. No network of tensions is created. Each tone refers primarily to itself, is responsible only to itself.

What broader intellectual structure corresponds now to this musical viewpoint? Palestrina works with separate tones, with elements which cannot be further subdivided. They do not permit us to look inside themselves; they possess no inner core. They can be compared to individual stones, which we can approach only from the outside; we can arrange them only from the outside. The basis of progression from one tone to the next does not lie within the tone itself, but rather comes from outside. This applies not only to the rhythmic—melodic relationship but equally to the sonority. Here, too, a question arises as to whether the individual tones which come together are compatible with one another. If they are not, there is a pressing need to move forward. But this pressing need arises from without. The progress of the individual melodic lines is determined by the vertical thrust. It is as if forward impetus in the compositional craft of Palestrina were brought about only by an external cause, just as water moves in obedience to the law of gravity or stones are set in motion by a kick or by the angle of the plane, without displaying any tendency towards motion within themselves. The compositional method of Palestrina is thus similar to an act of *nature*. It is like a symbol of nature, of lifeless nature. The individual element behaves in the manner of a lifeless object; it is set in motion by external influence. This influence, the cause of the motion, can be exactly determined, and so, as a result, can its effects as well. Thus everything that occurs in Palestrina's composition appears calculable, as if due to a law of causation. The compositional art of Palestrina provides an analogy to the methods of the established natural sciences. We discover in his music no orientation towards a goal, no inner intention, nothing teleological, no activity of the organism, no analogy with anything "organic." If, then, Palestrina's music gives a natural impression (see pp. 42 and 98) — if it is comparable to nature, to natural phenomena — this has its justification on deeper grounds. Palestrina's method of composition reminds us of crystal-clear water, of pure crystal, of a miracle of nature. It is not "alive," not "organic," but "natural."

As the second stage we can designate the period of the figured bass, the time approximately from 1600 to 1750. With Monteverdi and Schütz, for whom music is still identical with the setting of language, meaningful declamation of the text is of primary importance. In their works the distinguishing characteristics of the new stage do not appear in all their aspects with as much clarity as they do subsequently in the instrumental polyphony of Bach.

Using the example of the suspension, we have seen how a new synthetic manner of hearing could come into being which presupposes dissection into separate tones (see Exx. 49 and 50, above). A few further examples from Palestrina's works should serve to illustrate this. They are, so to speak, concessions; they transcend the strict rules. (As in the above examples, plain note-heads in Ex. 51 illustrate the mere juxtaposition of tones, whereas slurs refer to the necessity of listening in continuity.) Passages like Ex. 51a–d can be understood from the viewpoint of Palestrina; they can be heard according to the principles of his method of composition. At the same time, however, they can lead to the comprehension of new aspects, to the formation of new relationships. The tendency to hear such passages as a unit provides the starting point. In Ex. 51d the

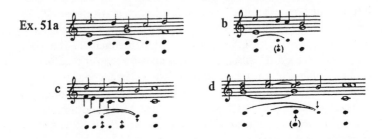

middle voice (c'') forms a fourth — that is, a dissonance — with the bottom voice (g') on the second half-note. In spite of this the note is tied over to the third half-note. This irregularity is made possible only by the even sharper dissonance which the upper voice (d'') now makes with it (interval of a second), by the resolution on the fourth half-note (b'), and by the stability of the bottom g', which has continued to sound since the first half-note. When the fourth half-note is reached, therefore, the listener must not have forgotten the first, and in fact, if the passage is to retain its meaning, the listener must be aware of all of the requirements just mentioned. The tendency towards comprehensive listening is further strengthened by the addition of a fourth voice: Ex. 52. Here it is the quarter-note f'

Ex. 52

which welds the tones even more firmly together by forming the interval of a tritone (an augmented fourth) with the $b\natural'$. It thus becomes necessary to hear the passage as a unified whole. In a unit of this kind there is a stirring of life. Strivings emerge, urging towards continuation in specific directions.

This sense of direction is linked in particular to the tritone. It occurs in the music of Palestrina, but it is not until the era of the figured bass that it is employed consistently; only here are its consequences realized. The tritone (e.g. *f–b*, and its inversion *b–f*) is a singular formation. It is the only sonority which occurs at one point only within the diatonic scale. It has an unmistakable contour which impresses itself on the memory; it forms a unit, which contains within itself, however, a clear propensity towards forward movement. It cannot rest within itself (it is not a consonance), but rather strives towards a goal. It combines within itself the two leading-tones (that is, those which lead into the next tone by means of a half-step) of the diatonic scale, and thereby it determines its resolution: Ex. 53. We can say that the cause of its unity is also the cause of its forward progression. The tritone was avoided in medieval music: it

Ex. 53

was known as the "diabolus in musica." This is understandable, for a tendency towards forward movement inherent in a sonority did not exist within the earlier view of music. The very characteristic, however, which formerly served to brand it "diabolus" now renders it popular. Let us remind ourselves, with reference to the tritone, of the transition which is taking place in listening to music. In Palestrina's music a given tone could form a passing dissonance or a suspension to another tone. The dissonance was formed externally, through the meeting of two independent tones, one as it were legitimate and the other in need of justification. In the case of the tritone this conception is of no help to us. It is not a question of the single tone being rendered dissonant by particular rhythmic–melodic circumstances, but rather of the tritone-sonority, as a unit, containing within itself, *intrinsically*, the cause of its forward progression. From now on the criterion is no longer dissonant versus consonant tone, but rather inherently static versus forward-striving sonority. For this same reason the term "dissonance" is inadequate when applied to the tritone.

The tritone functions as a ferment. It brings to lifeless "nature" the seed of organic matter. It infuses the other sonorities with life as well. Thus it joins forces with the well-established progression V–I to form the dominant seventh chord *g-b-d-f* (see Ex. 52 above). The *harmonic cadence* makes its appearance, a system whereby sonorities are combined according to their intrinsic tendencies, as shown in Ex. 54. Here it is not the individual tones (as in Palestrina's music) but the sonorities which are connected with one another. But now these sonorities are, as *chords*, the result of an abstraction: they are rationally determinable, that is, they are comparable to a perpendicular slice. They can also sound for a longer time without change.

Ex. 54 Bach, St. Matthew Passion

O Haupt voll Blut und Wun - den, voll Schmerz und vol - ler Hohn.

They are no longer identical with the sonorities of the Middle Ages, which comprised within themselves ornamentation (the later voice-leading), movement, fluctuation in time (see p. 97). The compositional process now unfolds through the combination of chords according to the principle of the cadence. The fact that the basis of composition now lies in the combination of chords finds expression in the technique of the figured bass (see also p. 73).

The new chordal concept also forms the prerequisite for the emergence of a secondary layer of ornamentation which is subordinate to the harmonic motion: Ex. 55. Thus in the polyphony of the

Ex. 55 Bach, Well-Tempered Clavier book I, C minor Fugue

thorough-bass era the formation of motives and sequential passages becomes, in contrast to the practice of Palestrina (see p. 98), vitally important – these features are strongly encouraged in the instrumental music of the seventeenth century. Ornamented chords and the tendency to listen to the whole rather than to specific details remind us of the irrational situation of polyphony before Palestrina. Now, however, they presuppose the stage represented by Palestrina's compositional method; they are refined by it.

The cadence, to which the individual chords are attached, forms a dynamic unit, a system of tensions. Thus the chords lose the reposeful, static character of the earlier sonorities. They are made relative, set in relationship to one another. Everything strives toward a goal, the tonic chord, which alone brings repose. This orientation toward a goal, this compulsion with which the tonic chord thrusts itself into the center, creates what we call *tonality*. But only through the formation of a system of cadences leading into foreign keys does the tonality make a strong impression on us. These cadences are in their turn part of a higher unity. From the individual chord to the composition as a whole we consistently find a correlation between the part and the whole. The individual component takes on significance from the whole and vice versa. But this, too, is a characteristic of the "organic." We observed (p. 101) that Palestrina's music offers an analogy with the causality of the natural sciences. It is as if it were capable of being exactly determined. The comparability of the thorough-bass technique with the world of the organic precludes this kind of causal determination. Musical structure here offers an analogy to the teleological methods of biology. For this reason the thorough-bass technique cannot be taught according to exact rules.

This stage has but one feature in common with the music of Palestrina, namely the fact that the structure of the composition unfolds continuously. The new way of listening is still contingent upon Palestrina's method of composition (see pp. 101f). The individual chords are not employed as ready-made symbols, but rather emerge in each case out of the polyphonic voice-leading. They are, however, no longer the chance result of the voice-leading, for their significance now depends on their function, their placement within the cadential structure. The composer specifically strives to achieve certain chordal progressions. The polyphony of the thorough-bass era is a *harmonic* polyphony. It was decisively encouraged by the formation of an instrumental—tectonic manner of thinking. (We are, however, unable to treat this important theme here. Compare also pp. 72f and 104). The instrumentalization of music by Bach, which is based on the synthesis of components from Monteverdi's technique with instrumental music, is thus closely connected with the formation of the mature thorough-bass practice of the time of Bach.

We can now apply a variation of what was said about Palestrina (see p. 101). The musical structure of the thorough-bass era is not a "natural" but rather a "living" phenomenon, resembling a living organism. Thus this music cannot be likened to a cool, quietly flowing, pure stream of water. Rather, the vision of warm blood pulsing through the veins forces itself upon us (cf. Ex. 54 above). The distance separating listener and work which characterizes the music of Palestrina is here no longer present. The new musical structure, as the image of the living creature, becomes of immediate concern to us, it seems to be a part of us. This music has, as it were, a commitment to flavor, whereas that of Palestrina resembles pure water with no taste. The music of Palestrina could realize only the objective aspect of the idea presented by the language (compare the discussion of *descendit*, pp. 43f and Ex. 23); the thorough-bass era sets the language as an expression of affect, as the cry of suffering (see also p. 49). The famous affect-laden musical gesture of Ex. 56 can stand as an epigraph over the entire thorough-bass period.

Ex. 56   Monteverdi, *Lamento d'Arianna*

Monteverdi's accomplishment cannot, to be sure, be understood solely through the inherently musical mastery of his technique. The renewal of music around 1600 is unthinkable without the direct stimulus which came to it through the word. Musicians discovered the word as a vehicle of emotion. This in turn contributed decisively to the awakening and furtherance of possibilities, which slumbered within the musical structure, of representing the organic. (Not until the minor triad was heard from the standpoint of the organic could it, too, be connected with the concept of suffering, an idea not associated with it in earlier times.)

The conception of "coming from within" which is attached to the new musical art and which was strengthened in particular by the German language (see p. 51) also finds its justification in the organic quality of the thorough-bass technique. As an example of this musically determined subjectivity we could present any of Bach's four-voice chorales, such as those in the Passions (see Ex. 54, above).

Let us, however, remind ourselves of yet a further characteristic of thorough-bass polyphony. It unfolds continuously (see p. 105).

When once set in motion, it moves forward compulsively, not to come to rest until the final chord. It is as if the continuation to the goal were latent within it at any given point; as if the beginning already contained within itself the entire passage. The composition functions as the actual realization of this latent material, as its projection along the axis of time. What is presented in the execution of the movement corresponds to our expectations. Only that occurs which can be predicted. Here time is not an independent dimension. It appears rather as the unfolding of that which is already present. A conceptual structure of this kind knows no division into past, present and future; it envisions the world as timeless, as consisting of the unproblematic ever-present. Its progression appears inevitable. This reminds us of the viewpoint of the prophet, who need only project his own reality onto some point in time to render actually present what is latently existent, for the purpose of unraveling what we call the future. This stance corresponds to the epic. (One could also, perhaps, compare the structure of Bach's music and the epic viewpoint in general to the idea of the conditionally determined will, as propounded, for example, by Leibniz. Similarly, one is reminded of Leibniz's views on analytical judgment and on the metaphysically determined concept of the subject, which includes implicit within itself all that can be expressed through a predicate. See, for example, Leibniz, *Discours de Métaphysique*, § 8.)

The question of the epic is also discussed in an exchange of letters between Schiller and Goethe (April, May, December 1797). Goethe observes that in the *Odyssey* the propitious outcome has been repeatedly foretold, "that the reader can know, indeed must know, the outcome of a good [epic] poem and that it is really the *how* which should hold his interest. As a result curiosity plays no role in a work of this kind, and its purpose can lie in each detail of its movement." (22 April 1797) In drama, however, it is not permissible to omit the moment of surprise, to anticipate the end effect. Further inquiry is conducted into the various characteristics which determine the difference between epic and drama, which Goethe must respect when composing his epic poems. Seen from the viewpoint of Schiller and Goethe this is justified. For today's viewer, however, there emerges a further aspect. The difference cannot be determined from characteristics of style alone, but is rather dependent to an essential degree on language, on the human—intellectual outlook of language. This primary layer, the structure of the vessel of meaning (in language as in music), is not accessible to human caprice; it remains untouched by the employment of either an epic or a dramatic representation of events. It is in each case the sum total, the result, of its own history. It is not left to the individual to extract the impossible from this layer. We cannot decide freely whether to compose epic or dramatic poetry. The creative act consists rather in the voluntary submission which allows us to produce actual results from the possibilities contained within the vessel of meaning. Just as tragedies could not have been written in the time of Homer, so the fifth century B.C. could not have brought forth valid epic poetry. The epic of Homer finds its analogy in the above-mentioned outlook of the prophet. Because of this the epic event strikes us as something unbroken, undivided, as though determined by a higher power.

Bach's music affects us in a similar manner. Thus the Bach Passion also exhibits an epic quality, even in its subject matter. There are no sudden surprises. We know the outcome, it is foretold, and Christ himself is aware of it. We find here the stance of the prophet. Through the music this is captured in an objective form. We must not, as sometimes happens, compare the Passion to drama simply because it expresses sublime suffering. As an image of the living creature the thorough-bass technique is capable of expressing suffering and passion. The characteristic peculiar to drama, however, is action (the Greek word *dráma* means "action"). Let us think for a moment of the chorale prelude *Vor Deinen Thron* (see pp. 76ff). Bach's music, that creation thoroughly pervaded by the human spirit, has indeed arrived at the stage of speaking, but it still thrives in the fertile soil of the naive, folklike chorale melody; it is nurtured by genuine naiveté. And in this respect too it retains something of an epic quality: what it conveys to us is like a real situation; not a mere illustration, not mere art or poetry in the usual sense.

The speaking quality of Bach's instrumental polyphony and the attitude of genuine naiveté join forces with the identification between subject and work which characterizes the stage of the organic (see pp. 105f). Thus Bach's music reminds us sometimes of simple prose,[31] such as that of the Gospel or the Lord's Prayer; it reminds us of confession or of prayer. The music of Bach makes possible, uniquely, an attitude of prayer. Perhaps the most convincing example of this is his last work, the chorale prelude *Vor Deinen Thron*.

Let us turn our attention to the third stage, to the musical language of the Viennese classical composers. In so doing we continue from the remarks made in the previous chapter (pp. 84–91).

There we proceeded from the observation that Viennese classical music is to be understood as the capturing of specifically human *action*. We are witness to an event which is taking place here and now in our presence, no matter whether it is a stage work or instrumental music. The structural characteristic of this approach to music is *discontinuity*, as we found it in Haydn's first string quartet. We experience no steady development. The chords do not emerge from the voice-leading as in the continuum of harmonic polyphony (see p. 105). Rather, they are employed as symbols within the cadence structure, having been saturated with meaning through centuries of polyphonic use. The thorough-bass is not compatible with this new attitude; it is abandoned.

With respect to the rondo theme from Haydn's quartet op. 33 no. 2, we observed the effects of discontinuity in mature Viennese classical music. Here it is employed so flexibly that we scarcely notice it. And yet we can only understand the structure properly if we envision it as compiled out of various elements, as it were physically compact, each introduced by a separate new impulse. We find it necessary to remain constantly alert in order to adjust our response to unexpected turns. Unlike what occurs with Bach or Palestrina, there suddenly emerge here in the course of the movement, as if from nowhere, *unforeseen* impulses which determine and shape the action. (Whereas the thorough-bass technique could be likened to Leibniz's concept of the subject – see p. 107 – the structure of Viennese classical music provides an analogy to Kant's synthetic judgment, in which the predicate goes beyond what is contained in the concept – that is, in which something is added to the concept during the process of forming a judgment.) This music thus contains within itself the necessity for an attitude identified with *conducting*. There now arises for the first time a music which inherently demands to be conducted. This new vessel of meaning operates with sudden surprises; it is not an epic but rather a dramatic language. It creates musical *theater*.

The attitudes of conducting and theater have a further sequel: they create a *vis-à-vis*, they create distance. When I observe someone in action in front of me, in my presence, I interpret this event as something outside of myself. It is real, but it does not coincide with the reality of my own person. Those are people of flesh and blood who are living and operating out there on the stage. But they do not belong to my own field of operation; they are *presented* to me. The naive belief "that's the way it was," which characterizes the epic

attitude, no longer exists here. In one sense the stage is more real
than the epic, for I experience living persons; in another sense, however, it is less real, for I know that this event is only imagined, that it
is only being presented to me. In the reality of the theater a *vis-à-vis*
is created for the specific situation and therefore is constituted in
whatever manner its creator deems appropriate. The theater is, as it
were, an experimental station. One seeks each time to find the
experimental method best suited to demonstrating an event as
taking place in the present — that is, to presenting it as theatrical
reality, as discontinuity.

The practice of focusing on the listener which the creation of that
vis-à-vis brings with it results in yet another trait of Viennese classical
music: its radiant energy. This is substantially strengthened by
differentiations in dynamics and tempo, which heighten its ability to
sweep us along in its path. These changes are consciously applied as a
compositional technique; they are set down in notational form.

But the all-embracing characteristic of classical compositional
technique — the one we took as our point of departure — is the
immediacy of the event taking place, and thus its discontinuousness,
the compilation of a passage from small, independent impulses. As a
result we must pose the question: what is it that brings about unity
in spite of constant change? What changes is the content, the
arrangement of rhythmic values and tones; what remains constant is
the metrical distribution of weights, the measure. For example, the
alternation between downbeat and upbeat impulses, an essential
aspect of Viennese classical music, is dependent thereon. (It is
impressive that at the end of Beethoven's life-work and thus of
Viennese classical music as well, downbeat and upbeat are set against
one another in epigrammatic fashion — see p. 54). Out of one and the

same rhythmic pattern — for example ♩ 𝅗𝅥 — can be created either a

downbeat (| ♩ 𝅗𝅥) or an upbeat (♩ | 𝅗𝅥) motive, depending on its

relationship to the measure (see also pp. 52f). We are here also
reminded of the metrically varying application of the harmonic progression dominant—tonic (see p. 88). The element which brings
about unity in all of these cases is the new, clarified concept of the
measure.

We might even say that the rational achievement of the classical
composers lies in the division of what had up until then been considered a unity between rhythmic—tonal contour and metric distri-

bution of weight into two independent elements which could be treated separately. As a result of this the human mind reached a new stage in its grasp of musical meaning and attained a new relationship to the world as music; as a result of this the technique of music was transformed. To this can be attributed the unique character of Viennese classical music. The measure had established itself in the instrumental music of the thorough-bass era (see p. 76), but only the musical technique of the Viennese classical composers carried this through to its logical conclusion and created the pure concept of the measure, the naked system of relationships. Just as the German language represents the antithesis of the Greek (see pp. 4f, 49f and 75), so Viennese classical music appears as the final stage in the formation of rhythm since the time of antiquity. Whereas Greek rhythm was founded on the concept of intrinsically 'filled-in time' (see p. 5), it remained for the Viennese classical composers – and for them only – to draw the ultimate conclusion from the separation between measurement of time on the one hand and its filling-in with content on the other.

Let us examine, finally, the beginning of the march from *The Magic Flute*: Ex. 57. Here we find, within the confines of an outwardly simple format, the classical principle of independent elements carried out consistently: every second measure introduces a new impulse, a new substance with its own form and its own will. The

Ex. 57

first section consists of four heterogeneous two-measure elements: the first beginning with a downbeat, in half-notes, complete in itself; the second beginning with an upbeat, in quarter-notes, forward-moving; the third again downbeat, but as a result of its melodic breadth and dotted eighth-notes now flowing, pressing onward (up to the last moment – the final eighth-note in m. 6); the fourth also downbeat, precisely pointed as a result of the dotted eighth-note, but complete in itself; with a sudden backward-throwing jolt, which springs up unexpectedly out of nowhere, it wipes out the forward-pressing movement of the third element. (A structure of this kind is reminiscent of the *contrapposto* of classical sculpture.)

This variegated diversity of shapes is kept under control by the outwardly smooth, almost folklike structure of two-measure symmetry. Behind it, however, is the new concept of the measure. This measure, now freed of all material content, is able to hold the heterogeneous elements together just because of this lack of any substance which might clash with them. It functions as a pure system of relationships which creates unity only in the mind's eye. This represents, however, the ultimate abstraction possible within a craft: to operate with a factor which has become pure form (in Kant's meaning), which has rid itself completely of substance. We are reminded that the same year, 1781, which marks the beginning of the mature classical period (Haydn's quartets op. 33 and Mozart's *Abduction from the Seraglio*) also brought the Kantian pure forms of perception, i.e. space and time; and it seems reasonable to appeal to the concept of absolute time and that of the absolute measure as parallel turning points in the intellectual—cultural history of Western civilization.

How thoroughly has musical structure been permeated by the human intellect! The march from *The Magic Flute* evokes in us a singular sense of intellectual activity, of the spontaneity of intellectual forces. Indeed, these self-willed, compact elements, which cannot be justified on either a causal or a final basis but rather enter freely each time, appear as the emblem of intellectual freedom, the emblem of man's free will. It was left to Viennese classical music to realize man in his singularity — that which is most specifically human, free will, human action — to represent all of these through musical means. In no other music, either preceding or following the Viennese classical masters, is this specific concern, or anything even similar to it, inherently contained.

The classical structure, composed out of independent elements, symbol of free will, can only be realized as a unity in our own imagination; only through the perceiving subject does it become meaningful. The unity is not contained, as for example in the music of Bach or Palestrina, in the sphere of discernible musical substance, of the objective—musical event, but is created only in a sphere completely abstracted from the object (in this case from the music), the purely intellectual sphere of the spontaneity of our inner being: in the unity, bare of all concrete substance, of our perceiving consciousness. The freedom of the Viennese classical masters is the freedom propounded by Kant: it is realized by attaining the last possible point of departure from which meaning in its absolute sense can still be grasped. This last foothold is the "*unity of apperception.*" This requires, however, the ultimate exertion of our person, our powers of apperception, our mental activity. The Viennese classical masters pursued conceptualization in the application of musical techniques so far that they reached the outermost confines of musical possibility. The next instance, from which the work can still be comprehended as autonomously meaningful, is the purely conceptual, which has no analogy in musical substance. One step further, and debilitation of the musical language as autonomous language is the result.

One last trait of classical music: as we observed above, the epic attitude corresponds to a kind of music in which a process of continuous unfolding is inherent. Past, present and future there form an unbroken whole. Time is not realized as an independent element (see p. 107). The classical format, on the other hand, which corresponds to the attitude of the theater, is discontinuous; in the course of its progress unexpected forces intervene which alter its movement. In classical music *time* can no longer be calculated in advance. We become conscious of it as an independent element. The Viennese classical technique consists in our becoming conscious of time. Temporality forces its way in. Through the emphasis on the here-and-now, that former epic unity has broken apart into present and future. Only Viennese classical music comprehends the consecration of the moment. Only here can movements be composed like "Die Stunde schlägt" ("The hour strikes") from *The Magic Flute* or "O Gott! Welch' ein Augenblick!" ("O God! What a moment!") from *Fidelio* or the *Et homo factus est* ("And was made man") from the *Missa Solemnis* (see p. 96). In passages like this beats the heart of Viennese classical music.

The repeated phrase *Die Stunde schlägt* in the second half of the trio "Soll ich dich Teurer nicht mehr sehn?" (*The Magic Flute*, no. 19) is sung by Sarastro. The entire number is sung *piano* with the exception of Sarastro's final *die Stunde schlägt*. Even this semi-divine being (who has previously announced the same phrase three times, always *piano* and rising chromatically every two measures: bb-$b\natural$-c-$c\sharp$-d), now loses his composure; he enters after just *one* measure, in his highest range and *forte*. The awareness of the present moment and thus of the event actually taking place is made visible in an all-consuming fervor, a force scattering all before it. It is like a bolt of lightning laying bare the innermost substance, suddenly lighting up the scene, whereby meaning manifests itself in the shape of the eternal as the present, as the irretrievable instant. The inner self can scarcely endure that. The coloratura sung by Pamina and Tamino follows in a kind of stammered delirium, and Sarastro's *Wir sehn uns wieder* ("We shall meet again") now comforts us mortals, fills us with extreme confidence after that manifestation of the god. We could even say that the classical composer finds meaning in the affirmative knowledge of the temporal. The awareness that the transitory is incompatible with the permanent (that is, with meaning), the affirmative knowledge of this antinomy, is the basis of tragedy. The wisdom of the tragic is the distinguishing mark of the classical master. It has been realized in music only once in the history of Western civilization, in Vienna in the period between 1781 and 1828.

Western music has carried out, on its own terms as it were, the process of the Creation. In the constant confrontation of the sonority with the word from Carolingian times up to Palestrina it had found itself. Then it traversed the stages of nature and of the organic. And thus it arrived at the final stage: its structure became the symbol of the human spirit of freedom. Now the aging Haydn could in *The Creation* validly extol mankind:

> Mit Würd' und Hoheit angetan
> Mit Schönheit, Stärk und Mut begabt
> Gen Himmel aufgerichtet
> Steht der Mensch, ein Mann und König der Natur
>
> (With dignity and nobility crowned,
> With beauty, strength and courage gifted,
> Towards Heaven raised up
> Stands mankind, as man and king of Nature.)

Only Haydn, the creator of Viennese classical music, had obtained the inner justification, only he could employ an adequate musical language, to create mankind anew through music, to represent him in a form corresponding to that of a full-bodied work of sculpture.

13 · The Romantic Era

Schubert, Beethoven's younger contemporary, lived and worked in the city of the Viennese classical composers, and he is also clearly related to them in his cultural–intellectual outlook. This applies in particular to the great Schubert as composer of German Lieder. He presupposes the classical musical technique, the format based on action. Other characteristics, however, distinguish him from the classical masters: classical music creates a *vis-à-vis*. In the aria "Voi che sapete" from Mozart's *Figaro* Cherubino explains his lovesick state by setting up his feelings as it were at a point opposite himself and allowing them to parade past as an event presently taking place. Schubert, in contrast, identifies himself with his Lied (as, for example, in *Winterreise*). In this respect he belongs to the Romantic era. (Thus on this point the Romantic composer exhibits characteristics related to the outlook of the thorough-bass era, whereas the classical composer more nearly resembles Palestrina; see pp. 106 and 109f). Schubert's Romantic side comes forward undisguised in works such as his Masses. We will therefore use his Mass in A flat major to illustrate the Romantic in music.

Let us compare it with a Viennese classical work, Beethoven's Missa Solemnis. The approach which views the word as action presently taking place leads in the *Dona nobis pacem* from the Agnus to that warlike episode with drums and trumpets which makes the cries of *miserere* and *dona nobis pacem* appear almost physically real. The movement carries the inscription given to it by Beethoven himself: "Bitte um innern und äussern Frieden" ("Prayer for inner and outer peace"). What does this mean? Why did Beethoven choose this inscription? This, too, appears as the result of that singular outlook which interprets the word as an event presently taking place, as action. For we could say that within this view the word originates at that point where the inner self encounters the outer world. Here the inner world cannot exist without the outer world, nor the outer world without the inner. This is the essential characteristic of Viennese classical music, a characteristic proper only to it. This craving of the inner self for objectification, for absorption of the outer world, also stamped the individuality of Beethoven's composition and gave rise to the inscription "Prayer for inner and outer peace."

The particular bond between the inner self and the outer world also reminds us, however, of the observations which we have made about the German word (see p. 51). It appears indeed that only the Viennese classical masters bring about the adequate musical realization of the conceptual basis which is presented in the German language. For the character of the actually present (see p. 57) and the attachment to images of action (see pp. 59f) are likewise factors which were already pre-formed in the outlook proper to the German language.

The Romantic composers, however, did not think in this manner. The effective power of the word is for them not directly released through contrast of the inner self with the outer world. For them the word is expressive only of the subjective, of the inner world. Differently formulated, the word exists here musically not as objectification but as feeling. The feelings, the moods evoked by the text are transformed into music. Language is employed as a mere table of contents. The path to subsequent program music has been cleared.

Schubert's Mass in A flat major was composed in the years 1819–22 – in the same Vienna and at exactly the same time as Beethoven's Missa Solemnis. The *Quoniam tu solus sanctus* ("For Thou only art holy") from the Gloria may serve to illuminate the Romantic outlook. This passage follows the *miserere nobis* ("have mercy upon us") which establishes the musical mood. From this point forward the sentiment gradually shifts with the *Quòniam tu solus*: there is an intensification, a transformation of the mood culminating in *tu solus Dominus*.

In the analogous passage of Beethoven's work, nothing of this is to be found, neither the gradual transition from one sentiment to the next nor the intensification. What rules here is the word, which is realized musically as action taking place in the present. Following the *miserere nobis* one is confronted directly with something new at the entrance of the kettledrum. The freely spoken word takes on, as it were, objective force:

Quoniam tu solus sanctus   *Quoniam tu solus Dominus*

and so on.

The beginning of the Credo is likewise instructive. In Schubert's setting it is the particular mood of affirmation, the satisfaction in a firm faith, which is given expression. The text moves forward at an even pace; it forms a unified whole which falls into two symmetrical parts, an antecedent and a consequent:

Credo in unum Deum   factorem coeli et ter-rae.

Beethoven, however, declaims thus:

Credo, credo   in unum, unum Deum.

In the emphatic repetition of the word *credo* he is saying not merely "I believe" but rather "*I* believe"; by repeating the *unum* he is stating not merely "in one God" but rather "in the one and only God." We are reminded inescapably of Schütz (see p. 61f). Schütz set this passage:

Ich glaube an einen einigen Gott.

Let us also look at the passage *visibilium omnium et invisibilium* ("of all things visible and invisible"). Schubert sets it like this:

vi-si-bi - li-um omnium et invisi-bi - li - um.

Beethoven, on the other hand, thus:

vi - si-bi-li-um   omnium   et   et in - vi - si - bi-li-um

and Schütz thus:

alles was sichtbar und unsichtbar ist.

The emphasis on the word *et*; the differentiated, vigorous diction of *invisibilium*: these traits remind us of Schütz's setting. In both cases there is a declamation answerable to the language, a clarification of the word content: in Schütz, as vocal music; in Beethoven, as interpretation through the means of instrumental music as well.

To what, however, can we attribute the great difference between Schubert's Mass and Beethoven's Missa Solemnis? We can perhaps shed light on this question by taking into consideration two elements, the tradition of the service Mass and the new social structure to which it is directed.

In previous chapters we have emphasized the fact that, following

the emergence of independent instrumental music, deeper spiritual—
religious meaning could no longer be captured in the service Mass. It
is rather conveyed in works such as Bach's B minor Mass and
Beethoven's Missa Solemnis, which cannot be considered church
music in the narrow sense. Schubert and the early Romantic era link
up not with these works but rather with the tradition of the service
Mass, and in fact more nearly with the Mass of the pre-classical than
with that of the classical composers. As we have already observed
(see pp. 92f), it had become the custom during the eighteenth century
to seek in the Mass a pleasant atmosphere, one of Sunday festivity,
joyful and entertaining. This is what the early Romantic composers
encounter as current practice and it is from here that they proceed
along their own path. However, since they bring with them a new
tendency towards inner fervor and thus towards a mystically tinted
piety, they also change the character of the musical Mass. The
expression of the festive, of the pleasant and joyful, is transformed
by Schubert into the indescribable euphony of his music, into an
inner fervor which touches us directly. Schubert seems to be intoxi-
cated with the tones and with the harmony of the Kyrie. The Gloria
(*Allegro*) still presents the age-old contrast to the Kyrie. This is
further intensified, however, by the harmonic coloring, in that the
Gloria is written not in A♭ major or one of its related keys but
rather in E major. In spite of the sharply defined contours in which
the text is declaimed at the beginning, the main concern here is still
the musically agreeable. Thus Schubert repeats the opening *Gloria
in excelsis Deo* after *Glorificamus te* in order to achieve formal
musical unity, even though the continuation of the text *Glorificamus
te* ("We glorify thee"), with *gratias agimus tibi* ("we give thanks to
thee"), does not imply such a repetition. Completely different is
Schubert's relationship to text in his Lieder. A masterpiece such as
Winterreise, for example, in spite of its Romantic traits, reminds us
of the Viennese classical masters and must be viewed in relation to
the Mass we have just discussed, not only as more significant music
but as a work of a different compositional structure, which offers no
basis for comparison.

A second factor relevant to an understanding of the Romantic
Mass is the emergence of a new social structure. The music of earlier
times addressed itself to an aristocratic, or at least an exclusive,
circle of listeners; only from them did the composer expect genuine
understanding, and only in them could he assume the necessary
knowledge and the necessary tradition. The musician of the Romantic

era addresses himself, however, to a new audience, to an audience of an anonymity which could not have been conceived of in earlier times. The listener — the knowledgeable listener — can no longer be identified; one knows nothing about him, who he is, whence he comes. He is now known simply as a citizen. This middle-class society now fills the halls. In the church it seeks edification, comfort, salvation. Just as it is unable to prove its own identity and is ignorant of its own roots, so also it is incapable of understanding the work it hears as part of a tradition. It cannot comprehend the depth of a work's history but rather can only be affected by its radiant energy, can only enjoy it as an experience.

The liturgy of the Mass is likewise beyond the comprehension of the new society; for many it is something far removed, something silent. The worshiper is scarcely concerned with the liturgical event, with the word, but reads instead from his own private prayer book which has no direct relationship to the text of the Mass. The Mass is now merely the incentive to private devotion. What surrounds the worshiper is no longer the word as sound or even the intended meaning but rather a certain atmosphere. Within this atmosphere the word is perceived in music as a kind of indistinct mumbling. The main concern is not the sounding language, but rather the indeterminate—musical, the fervent, the exalting, the all-enveloping.

The Romantic era coincides with the epoch of the so-called Restoration, the time around 1830. It is significant that the church musicians of the Restoration do not attempt to continue along the path of the Viennese classical masters. They tend to view the sacred music of the classical masters rather as a decadent manifestation and attempt to link up with the older tradition. One of the most important representatives of this approach, Kaspar Ett in Munich, is in fact the pupil of musicians who continue the pre-classical tradition rather than coming from the Viennese school.

The anonymity of the new society also finds expression in the new organization of the musical institutions of the church. Church choirs began to be formed from volunteer members. Associations of church musicians — that is, of the middle-class laity — took over the responsibility for the cultivation of sacred music from now on and left their mark on it accordingly. The newly emerging conservatories developed a style of curriculum which attempted to do justice to the new ideals and which was open to all.

In the second half of the century significant works arise out of this new spirit. Masses such as those by Liszt and Gounod seem to be trying to lift up the dome of the church and lure down Heaven from above.

The opposite pole is represented by Bruckner. He, too, is a Romantic composer. However, since he not only lived but also worked in an unbroken tradition of Christian faith, since he created even his symphonies in this spirit and was active as an organist in the same spirit, he was able, alone of his generation, once again to compose Masses which achieve the same level as independent works of art as that of his secular compositions and yet still constitute sacred music in its narrower sense. The return to a liturgical outlook is also documented externally in his E minor Mass, in the use of only a small wind ensemble and also in the fact that Gloria and Credo begin after the intonation of the priest. The Gloria thus begins with the words *Et in terra pax* and the Credo with *Patrem omnipotentem*.

As a Romantic composer Bruckner proceeds in his compositions from the inner self, from the inner world. In his works we do not find that identity of inner and outer worlds which was characteristic of Beethoven. However, Bruckner responds to the Christian cult from the depths of his soul. This guides him in his comprehension of the word beyond the mere mood which it conveys, but yet restricts him to a subjective approach. It is therefore understandable that he is often called a mystic. The word as sound has in his works a binding force which is lacking in those of the other Romantic composers.

14 · The Present

We will devote this chapter to the music of the Mass in the contemporary scene, but not, as one might expect, to contemporary settings of the Mass alone. For the question, which we have also pursued in previous chapters, must be formulated: what changes has the musical interpretation of the Mass undergone in the course of its history, and at each period what particular musical realization of the Mass was generally regarded as authentic, as legitimate? If, therefore, we were to attempt here to treat only contemporary settings of the Mass, we should be unjustifiably restricting the scope of the investigation. For there can be no doubting that today it is not only contemporary settings which are viewed as valid interpretations of the Mass. In the public awareness, settings of the Mass from the past claim the right to an equal place alongside them. Among these Gregorian chant takes on particular importance. And with Gregorian chant is in turn connected a further phenomenon of the present, namely the liturgical movement. In considering Mass music in the present we will therefore bring together three particularly important factors: the contemporary setting of the Mass, the reinstatement of Gregorian chant, and the music of the liturgical movement.

The Mass by Stravinsky can serve as an example of contemporary Mass composition. It is, to be sure, not the work of a church musician. It does not belong in the tradition of the service Mass, about which we spoke earlier. Stravinsky's Mass is, however, the free creation of an exponent of contemporary music, the work of an extraordinary personality, and for precisely that reason it must be taken into consideration. For if we propose to follow the setting of the Mass in contemporary *art* music, we must confine ourselves to those composers who have decisively influenced the fate of composition.

What led Stravinsky, the composer of ballets, instrumental music and secular librettos, to compose a Mass? Clearly, the stimulus came from the Latin text, and from its fixed form which has outlived the centuries. Both convey the impression of the universally valid, of that which is limited by neither nationality nor time. For this reason Stravinsky had already chosen the Latin language as the basis of other works. The character of the authentic which distinguishes this supranational and supratemporal language intrigues him. For his music seeks to free itself of the intimate, the subjective, the individual. The musical tradition of the nineteenth century, however, is bound to just these traits and thus also to the vital national languages. Stravinsky's music does not conform to this "vital" quality. His music is rigid and insists on being rigid. For this reason the Latin language, that universally valid but dead language, is compatible with the ideal of musical expression which Stravinsky embraces. This language encourages him in his efforts to free himself from the musical tradition of the nineteenth century. For a nineteenth-century composer involved in setting the Mass the problem was how to reconcile the subjective, intimate and unfettered quality of that music with the inaccessible severity of the Mass form and the crystal-clear, chiseled and unyielding Latin language. For Stravinsky this formulation of the problem has been reversed, namely, how the composer can free himself from the subjective, informal qualities of the music and the setting of modern languages which have been handed down through tradition. And as a result he is drawn to the Latin language and particularly to the Mass. He does not approach the Mass through the liturgy; rather, he comes to the liturgy through his conception of composition. He confronts not the problem of the Mass which he must solve in some manner by means of compositional techniques but rather the problem of composition which he attempts to solve with the help of the Mass and its text. For this reason his work bears the stamp of the "artistic." In the course of our observations, however, we have seen that the Mass has not always been regarded as Stravinsky regards it. The rigid and the dogmatic were stressed particularly in the Middle Ages. Thus certain characteristics of the settings of that time are very apt for Stravinsky's Mass. Let us look, for example, at the *Et incarnatus* from the Credo: Ex. 58. And let us place next to it the corresponding passage from the Mass of Machaut (see Ex. 36, p. 67 above). The similarity is, however, restricted to the rigid declamation of the individual syllables and to their mechanical scansion. Otherwise Stravinsky is concerned

Ex. 58

with something different. For example, he pursues a closed structure not only within the individual movements but also for the Mass as a whole. The first threefold Kyrie forms an opening; it stands by itself as a closed entity.[32] The type of cadence which it uses has been adapted from classical music.

The smoothly flowing Christe with its imitation reminds us of the *a cappella* polyphony of the sixteenth century; the independent, sharply pointed instrumental accompaniment with its motivic character, on the other hand, is related to classical instrumental music.

The impressive restatement of the first few measures of the Kyrie at the close of the movement brings about a compactness similar to prototypes taken from the golden age of instrumental music.

The Gloria, too, invokes memories of the previously known — this time, however, of liturgical models: the melismatic solo voices recall the function of the prayer leader. They are followed by a diffuse, stagnant sound complex sung by the choir, which appears to have been picked up from the loud chanting of a church congregation, as it is still found today in the Catholic church in the recitation of the litany or of the rosary. The concluding *Amen* of the Gloria has the same effect.

The Credo also reminds us of the chanting of a church congregation, but this time without a leader. Instead, we are at times given the impression that men and women are alternating in their recitation as is the custom in the rosary. In this same Credo, however, we also find moments which are suggestive of other models. Thus there are passages whose musical setting must be understood from the meaning of the text. An example of this is the section *Et iterum venturus est cum gloria judicare vivos et mortuos: Cujus regni non erit finis* ("And He shall come again with glory to judge both the living and the dead, and His kingdom shall have no end"). Here the intensification called forth by the affect, which reminds us more of a fanatical crowd than of a church congregation, is dependent on the content of the text. The same holds true for the hammering-out of the word *Ecclesiam* at the end of the phrase *Et unam sanctam catholicam et apostolicam Ecclesiam* ("And [I believe] in one holy, catholic and apostolic Church").

The closing *Amen* with its imitation, however, transports us back to the world of art music. And yet we do not perceive this as a break; we do not look upon this *Amen* as a heterogeneous element but rather as the keystone of the Credo. In the Sanctus it is the free melodic ornamentation of the two to four solo voices singing simultaneously which attracts our attention. This calls to mind the improvised ornamentation typical of the early Middle Ages.

Throughout Stravinsky's Mass, then, we find elements reminiscent of earlier practices. And yet it does not present an effect of disunity. Unity is achieved through the conscious remodeling of these retrospective elements into rigid shapes. This basic attitude, however, is that of the polyphony of the early Middle Ages.

What distinguishes Stravinsky from this early practice is threefold. (1) His roots are not in the liturgy but rather in art; his music is consciously "artistic." From this vantage point he strives to evoke an impression of the firmly established, of the dogmatic. The concept of the cantus firmus — the inner necessity of employing a given liturgical melody in the composition — is lacking in Stravinsky's work. (2) He has at his disposal techniques from the entire history of music and not just those of the early Middle Ages. (3) The rigidity of the textual and the musical phrase in early polyphony formed a beginning stage, upon which later periods could build until they reached complete realization of the language as the image of man. That first stage led subsequently to Palestrina, to Schütz, to Bach, to Beethoven. It was *not yet* the complete image of man. At the opposite pole from this rigidity of the early Middle Ages, this "not yet," stands the rigidity of Stravinsky's Mass, a "no longer."

Stravinsky proceeds from questions of musical composition, and his music exhibits in the process a certain outward similarity to medieval polyphony. The second phenomenon of the present time upon which I should like to touch briefly, the reinstatement of Gregorian chant, represents a return to an even older epoch, a return to the Roman tradition of approximately the seventh and eighth centuries. The background of the efforts to revive Gregorian chant, however, is formed not by problems of composition but rather by the liturgy. An attempt is made to reintroduce that setting of liturgical texts which in its very essence and to its very roots formed a requisite part of the liturgy: for liturgy is, as we have seen, *sounding* language. It was this side of traditional liturgy, its sound, which one hoped to restore. Not only the texts but also the melodies which had been intertwined with them were accorded theological–liturgical significance. We have already observed this in connection with the adoption of the Christian liturgy by the Germanic tribes. We have seen that the Nordic races were obliged to retain the given melodies in the emergence of polyphony, because these melodies formed a necessary part of the liturgy. Even in the newer polyphonic settings the given melody had to be present as a cantus firmus, representing dogma. Thus the return to Gregorian chant in modern times presupposes the adoption of a strict liturgical standpoint. Only the traditional liturgy is accepted, and that as a unity of ritual, text and music. A new setting of the text — that is, music as a supplement to the liturgy — is unacceptable. Thus the reintroduction of Gregorian chant forms the opposite pole to the music of Stravinsky and to modern Mass settings in general. Whereas Stravinsky desires that his music should invoke the *effect* of the authentic statement, the proponents of Gregorian chant are looking for a musical setting which by virtue of its *origins* contains within itself the mark of authenticity.

The third phenomenon of the present, the liturgical movement within both the Protestant and Catholic confessions, also proceeds from the liturgy rather than from questions of musical composition when dealing with the music of the Mass. The very term "liturgical movement" is itself indicative of this approach. However, although it is connected through its origins with the strict liturgical standpoint of the Benedictine monks in their efforts to restore Gregorian chant, it does not pursue the same goal, but emphasizes instead the building-up of the community and thus the sociological point of view. Indeed, the liturgical movement too would like to return to the liturgy of earlier times. It attempts in fact to establish ties with a stage even earlier than that of Gregorian chant, namely with the early Christian era. But whereas the Benedictines desire to retain the form of the old liturgy itself as the only form which is valid by virtue of its origins — whereas, that is, they assume an aristocratic standpoint by detecting validity in historical roots — the liturgical movement seeks to extract from the early Christian liturgy only a mode of operation, namely the active participation of the community in the liturgical event. Thus it is not the fact of the historically given, in the sense of the "inviolable" or of the cantus firmus, which for the liturgical movement is decisive. For it is prepared to give up the traditional language and its mode of performance in pursuing its primary goal of building a new liturgical community. It introduces translations into the liturgy. In setting these to music the main concern is not the retention of Gregorian melodies — this is conceptually insignificant and even musically impracticable once the supporting vessel, the Latin language, has been abandoned — but rather the employment of melodies appropriate to the singing of the texts

by the modern congregation. The liturgical movement is thus related
to the Benedictine efforts in that it proceeds from liturgical considerations; in being sociologically oriented, however, it has something in
common with Stravinsky's approach, for it seeks the authentic not
in its *origins* but rather in its *effect*.

All three of these phenomena — Stravinsky's setting of the Mass,
the return to Gregorian chant, and the liturgical movement — have
one feature in common: the linking-up with early, long-past times.
Yet another phenomenon of the present age directs its gaze backward in time: the desire and the ability to perceive musical settings
from the entire historical past as valid interpretations of the Mass.
Yet whereas the other manifestations feel an affinity for only one
particular approach from the past, there appears here to be an open-
ness, a receptivity to all stages of history.

We may now rightly ask ourselves which of all these possibilities
is the truly valid one for our time. I would risk the reply: no single
one of them, taken by itself. For the intellectually concerned person
of today the valid sound of the Mass is not this or that particular
setting from the present or from the past but rather the whole of the
Mass settings, their sum total in the past and the present (see also
p. 68). All together they form the music of the Mass in the present.
The significance of the Mass as something to be heard, its obligatory
side, is not accessible to us as in earlier times, when only the contemporary setting constituted in each case the single valid approach, but
is rather contained for us of today, as it were, in the ideal, in the
attempted integration of the entire body of musical settings. In
other words, it is not just this chapter but rather the entire book
which has dealt with the present musical scene. This may also be
viewed as the deeper justification for its having been written.

15 · Music as History

What conclusions should be drawn from the final remarks of the previous chapter? Are we perhaps no longer as easily satisfied as in
earlier times, are we for this reason not content to limit ourselves to
the music of our own time, and do we wish instead to have at our
disposal as rich and colorful a variety as possible? Does this mean

that we lack a definite standpoint or that our creative energy is on the decline? Is this to be interpreted as historicism, relativism, eclecticism, classicism, quietism, or whatever term one wishes to give it? Or can this peculiar tendency of the modern age to see the essence of music only in the totality of historically accessible music be interpreted as a new and special kind of musical activity?

In the first chapter of this book ("Introduction") we referred to this complex of questions and to the change in outlook which accompanies them. Now that we have traveled the path of historical music, of "our" music, that observation, too, can be presented in greater detail and thus better understood.

European music, from the Carolingian era — and, in a broader sense, from antiquity — to the end of the Viennese classical period, forms a unified whole (see also pp. 23 and 111). Up to that point each new phase of music contained implicitly within itself the stages which had preceded it (see the example from Bach, pp. 76ff). The spirit of musical syntax, its structural framework, constituted, as it were, its historical memory. Thus the entirety of historical music is actively present in the works of the Viennese classical masters; music as the symbol of that which is specifically human represents the ultimate consequence in the formation of Western music.

There followed the deepest cleft in the history of music. Like the emerging middle class, the new music was characterized by a loss of memory (see also pp. 118f). Musical composition was no longer governed by historical roots but rather by effect (see also pp. 125f). Hitherto the musical vehicle of meaning had a structurally conceived framework. Only from the outside could it appear to be natural (see, for example, pp. 42 and 94). This purely external effect of its structure, however, was now looked upon as the essence of the musical work. In place of a valid substantive vehicle of meaning there arose a shadow, namely naturalism, the one-sided emphasis on the private and subjective, the egocentric, the individual experience.

This type of music thus emerged out of the given realities through transformation of the valid and substantive into the egocentric and shadowlike. Alongside it, however, there was another kind of music, new music in a stricter sense, which cannot be derived directly from the mainstream of Western tradition and which is thus permitted, as it were, to be unconcernedly naturalistic. Through Mussorgsky (*Boris Godunov* 1871), Bizet (*Carmen* 1875), and also Verdi (for example, *Otello* 1887) music received new impulses. By way of Debussy and Stravinsky these have remained active into the present time.

Stravinsky, however, also established connections once again with the older tradition of Western music, and in fact in a very peculiar manner. He shows a tendency to assimilate possibilities from all of the music of the past into his own style (see pp. 122f). This tendency, however, is not identical with the historical memory contained in the work of earlier periods. It is rather the result of the loss of that memory. What was formerly contained implicitly in the work is now to be added to it as the sum of separate, consciously determined elements. In this way the history of music is to be rendered useful to contemporary composition. What emerges from this is not something disunified and various. It bears the stamp of the creative personality. The cohesive element is the tendency to unite the history of music, as it has been handed down, with the composer's own musical techniques — which originate in that offshoot represented by Mussorgsky and Debussy; it is the desire to interpret the musical techniques transmitted through history in the light of the composer's own approach to the art, to see them as something which is valid today.

In certain works by Carl Orff we also find a peculiar relationship to the historical. He employs no librettos in the usual sense, no verbal texts as mere framework, no specially adapted subject matter, in order to compose independent music. He tends instead to use important works from Western cultural history in unaltered form as the basis of his compositions, employing musical techniques solely with the object of rendering those works accessible to us. It is his desire to present the *Carmina Burana* or *Antigone*, for example, in a form valid for our time. What emerges is to be understood less as an independent work than as a kind of stage direction. The definitive meaning which is captured in the given historical work desires to be *interpreted*. The work demands this of us. This calls to mind the cantus-firmus approach and the different valid musical interpretations of liturgically specified chant and of the dogma (see pp. 15 and 22f). In a similar way the music of the Mass interprets a meaning which is unalterable, yet which is objectified as both word and action; it interprets this as something valid for each particular era. It becomes evident that interpretation (that is, a work dependent on meaning which has already been given specific form) and free creation (that is, autonomous, independent work) cannot be rigidly distinguished from one another. The modern interpretative composition does indeed give the older outlook a new meaning in the sphere of the secular and the avowedly artistic. But the way to both of these was paved in the work of Bach (the instrumental–secular; see pp. 83f) and of the Viennese classical composers (the attitude of the *vis-à-vis*, of presentation to a public; see pp. 109f). Retreat was no longer possible.

But let us turn our attention to music history. Its goal is also interpretation, its path genetic change. Thus this book, too, strives to understand the formation and growth of music, to consider the whole of historical music as a unity (see also pp. 2f). It is as if the memory which was implicitly contained in musical works composed up until the time of Schubert's death in 1828 should now be explicitly described and analyzed in separate stages, as if music history were to demonstrate a tendency to compensate for what has been missing from music since 1828.

But music history cannot, if it is to interpret, disregard the observer. It tries to represent the meaning which it interprets as something which is valid *for us*. Only within this self-limitation can it render the meaning accessible to us. That is, to be sure, a prerequisite governing every interpretative or historical discipline. For music history, however, it holds true to a greater extent and in unique fashion. For musical interpretation culminates in the actual realization of sound. To produce sound is the ultimate goal of the music historian (see p. 27). The meaning of the work is contained not in the silent notation alone but rather in the synthesis of notation with concept of sound. Notation and concept of sound are two different things (see pp. 26f). Thus even a particular contemporary interpretation (for example, the fiction of a recording of Bach's music from his own time, or even played by Bach himself) is not to be identified with the composition as set down in notation. Even then — and even though it may be regarded as authentic — its relationship to the composition is that of the individual case, the example, to the universal, and it has all of the advantages and disadvantages of the finitely determined, of that which has been fixed in one particular manner.

But in the case of *historical* interpretation the independence of the realization in sound, as opposed to notation, is strengthened by the appearance of yet a further variable dimension: to the notation which has been handed down to me from the past I add the actual tone, something which can be real only in the present; I produce sound. This sound is properly mine. The tonal phenomenon is a manifestation in time, a manifestation of the "inner meaning" (to use Kant's terminology), and is thus bound inescapably to the

present. A sounding tone is only my own presence. To be sure, it
may have been prompted by a historical concept of sound; indeed, it
is necessary to employ certain facts gleaned from the past with as
much accuracy as possible. The question of musical interpretation,
however, is not simply a search for the historically accurate sound,
but at the same time for that sound which has *validity* for us; or,
better, the search for the historically accurate sound insofar as it can
be considered to be valid for us. This validity is connected with our
own professional musical (for example, technical) as well as cultural
and sociological background, with rational and technical–physical
prerequisites as well as with the perceiving personality. In the
interpreted work various components are identifiable: the historically
given and the new as created by us; the historical notation and the
sound as presented by us; the past and our own selves. Between
these two layers there exists as mediator an ideal, not yet objectified,
very vague conception of the historically given elements of sound.
The attempt to reconstruct the presumed historically accurate sound
does not in itself lead to the goal (as in the so-called study of performance practice, or in performances of old music which purport to
be historically faithful). Only a music-historical interpretation can
integrate the work, insofar as it advances in each case to actual
execution on the basis of the given prerequisites and presents the
work in the form of sound which is valid for our present time. Then
it is an interpretative realization of something which has been placed
in our care and not an imitation of something out of the past.

In this way music-historical interpretation, like interpretative
composition, takes on something of the outlook of earlier times (see
p. 128). There is, to be sure, an essential difference: not only is the
music-historical interpreter bound to the notation, but it is also his
avowed purpose to fulfill his mission as historian by doing justice to
the work, by realizing as nearly as possible what is inherent in the
composition. The freely creative aspect of this activity follows
automatically — we could almost say, against the music historian's
will — as the result of the above-mentioned restriction: that the
music-historical interpretation (and this means the theoretical as well
as the practical) can, in a particular way, be valid only for our own
time. Let us take notice of yet a further difference between our
approach of today and that of the past. For the composer of earlier
periods the given cantus-firmus idea was something timeless, which
stood outside the stream of history; as a result his work had something static about it. The contemporary individual interpretation,

however, finds itself in interaction with the dynamic—historical out-look, which seeks the idea in the interpretation of the historical, in historical unity.

Another characteristic, however, connects this interpretation with the musical practice of past ages: since its purpose is explicitly that of demonstration, the character of an independent work does not adhere to it. This reminds us of early polyphony, which must be viewed less as an independent composition than as a way of pre-senting the given liturgical chant (see p. 17). It was intended to serve only for the present time; its character was improvisational, with nothing of the monumental about it. This, however, connects it to our own time. For today we find validity in solutions which simply desire to serve present needs, whereas the claim to monumentality — for example in contemporary compositions which profess to be independent, lasting work — arouses our suspicion.

Is there, however, a genetic explanation for this turn towards music history? I think there is an explanation to be drawn (a) from music history as a specialty, (b) from the history of philosophy, and (c) from Western cultural—intellectual history in general.

(a) Viennese classical music created certain inner prerequisites, which fostered the emergence of the outlook peculiar to music-historical interpretation. The formation of a *vis-à-vis* and the emergence of the conductor's role were characteristics of Viennese classical music (see pp. 109f). The conductor was an eminent per-sonality who dedicated himself purposely to interpretation, at that time of course primarily to that of contemporary music. Nonethe-less, both of these aspects, the creation of a *vis-à-vis* and the task of interpretation, are essential to music history. In addition we found a characteristic of Viennese classical music in the fact that composers became conscious of time as an independent factor (see p. 113). This was the first music to grasp the independent aspect of the temporal through musical means — here, to be sure, still as something present, as drama, as tragedy. But the element of the temporal, now seen as formation, is essential to the understanding of music as history. The succession of musical manifestations can only attract our attention when an awareness exists of time as formation. That tragic awareness of the incompatibility of the momentary with the permanent (see p. 114), the incompatibility within the simultaneous, forms the prerequisite for the historical awareness of the incompatibility of consecutive temporal manifestations among themselves, the incom-patibility within the successive.

But the interpretation of historical music is bound in yet another way to the awareness of time. The central question of music-historical interpretation is that of the tone ideal, as it is objectified in the vehicle of meaning. We ask ourselves how the tone ideal is altered, what kind of integration the inner self enters into with the tone in each case, what the tone has meant to the inner self in the course of history. But the tone ideal is merely a manifestation of time. The speculative central question of the music historian is thus that of the time ideal. He must interrogate music history with regard to the possibilities of combining elements of time and filling in spans of time (compare, for example, the various ways in which the question is posed in this book, in particular the change from the intrinsically filled-in time of Greek antiquity to the distinction drawn in Viennese classical music between pure time measurement and its filling-in with content: see pp. 110f). An awareness of the variable nature of the time ideal was awakened in the musician only by the music of the Viennese classical composers.

(b) With our inquiry into the time ideal we have, however, entered the realm of philosophy. I do not propose to remain there for long. I would simply call to mind the fact that Kant, who found his own access to philosophy in the activity of the perceiving subject, and who understood time as a form of intuition, became as a result the last philosopher who was still able to comprehend reality as something static, something ahistoric. For idealism, which sought to materialize not only that activity of the intellect which had become visible but even the intellect itself, was obliged to watch the static intellect as such disintegrate and transform itself into change and growth. It seemed that from now on meaning could only be grasped as growth. Hölderlin carried this out as a poet. He also raised it to the level of consciousness. "To understand the language of the Gods, change and growth" − these are words to which generations would be indebted. Hegel realized it as a philosopher. But just as there was no music of equally high rank to follow the Viennese classical masters, so Hegel found no successor of equal stature. The true successor to Hegel is in fact Ranke, who, considering his specialized historical background, must seem to be Hegel's opposite pole. And at that time it was not a philosopher, but rather a historian, Droysen, who had significant thoughts about the fundamental concepts of history (*Grundriss der Historik*, 1868). In formulations such as "What the generic concept is to animals and plants − for the genus consists in ἵνα τοῦ ἀεὶ καὶ τοῦ θείου μετέχωσιν ('their being part of the eternal and the divine') — that is history to mankind," we can glimpse once again the relationship between the cultural—intellectual outlook of the historian and that of the Viennese classical masters (see pp. 109ff). The discipline of history had taken over from philosophy the tendency to view history as a unity. It was therein that Ranke perceived what was distinctive in his way of viewing history (*Über die Epochen der neueren Geschichte* (On the Epochs of Modern History), 2nd lecture). Only in the attempt to grasp the manifestations of history as a totality did there emerge a meaning which could hold them together.

The concern of music history should be understood on a similar level. Now that the particular, as it were static, realization of the concept of music has come to an end — now that the perceiving subject has, through the work of the Viennese classical masters, been called upon as the final authority (see pp. 112f) — now it is time to effect a reversal in the manner of looking at things as well: music is, so to speak, the dynamic continuity of the historical forms of musical manifestation, which are among themselves mutually exclusive. The essence of music, the unity, lies in the act of understanding this growth and change as the unfolding of a meaning which cannot be grasped as a separate entity.

With this the self-evident aspect of tradition and of interpretation ceases to exist; access is gained to the compositions of the past which have been set down in written form. The golden age of naive creation has come to an end. Since man's intellect consistently seeks unity, it can now find such unity only in the synthesis of the historical forms in which music has manifested itself. (This integration is present only in the subject, only in the *act* of understanding.) Tone as formation and growth is the present-day form of the tone ideal; music as history, the present-day form of music.

(c) A general cultural-historical consideration also contributes to the genetic explanation of the interpretational approach. It does not appear to have penetrated deeply enough into the consciousness of the general public that Kant's critique of aesthetic judgment offers less a philosophy of the beautiful or even of art than a philosophy of the particular as opposed to the conceptual—universal. Viewing it from this perspective we can say that a static—dogmatic definition of art is not appropriate. It is true that there always exists an intellectual—cultural attitude which seeks to grasp the particular as such. It corresponds to the object of Kant's aesthetic judgment. However, its standing is higher than that of art in the narrower sense;

it contains more possibilities. What we generally understand under the term "art" is in fact the Western manifestation. This art of Western civilization presupposes something which lies outside its own boundaries. Western music exhibits a relationship of this kind, for example, with regard to the word as the embodiment of meaning, as faith made visible (see pp. 3 and 7f). Similarly, the poetry of the Western world presupposes simple prose as its ultimate source (see pp. 5f), the prose of the religious foundation and of the Gospel.[33] Without a relationship of this kind Western art becomes meaningless, it loses its binding validity. To express it in a way which seems paradoxical, the aesthetic autonomy of the vehicle of meaning (that is, of the work of art) becomes possible only as a result of this, its genetic dependence.

The ancient Greeks, however, knew nothing of such a manifestation. In their works the poetic—perceptible reality of art and religious content of truth are bound up in one; they form an indissoluble unit (see p. 8). It is in this sense that we must understand their term *musiké* (see pp. 6f). Not only can this not be translated simply as "music," but it cannot even be termed "art" in our sense. Our Western art presupposes the field of tension which is formed between the word and art, between language and music. The *musiké* of antiquity, however, does not recognize this distinction. In it language as unalterable meaning and music as art form a unity. Such a vehicle of meaning is an autonomous substance. It is not, however, an autonomous artistic—aesthetic object in the Western sense. It is binding on the very essence of man in his totality, on that which the Greeks called *ethos*; it determines man's essential quality, namely his ability to take action; it is present as an active factor; it has *representative* power. In contrast the Western work of art had the power to *eradicate* the object, the power to create the object anew as an artistic—aesthetic reality. I say "had," for it appears that this intellectual—cultural attitude which can be termed "creative" in a special sense has reached its conclusion with the end of the great tradition in Western music, philosophy and poetry around 1830.

It would, however, be false to assume that the human intellect, that hydra-headed creature, had simply capitulated. It appears that it is now in the process of developing from within itself a new possibility of grasping the particular as such. It is true that the word no longer possesses a representative power, nor does it have the power to eradicate the object; in place of this, however, it is developing a new, previously unknown power, namely that of *witnessing* or pointing out. Since language has become helpless as a force working to eradicate an object, it has with inner wisdom retracted itself to the function of bearing witness. By joining itself anew to the object, it is able to draw on new power and to compose itself, as it were. The witnessing power that St. John saw in the word is now brought into the foreground. (History "is not 'the light and the truth,' but rather the search for them, a sermon on them, the consecration of them: for as in St. John's Gospel, 'He was not that Light but was sent to bear witness of that Light.' " – Droysen, *Grundriss der Historik*, § 86.) This intellectual–cultural outlook, which encompasses the new art as well as historical interpretation, appears to be characterized by this activity of explaining, of pointing out; it seeks to comprehend intellect as history and as memory, and in this way to bring about an expansion of our awareness.

The interpretative outlook, however, also has, as it were, an ethical mission. For the historical object desires to live, to continue working. But left alone it is helpless. We must reach out to it, extend it our hand. It can only live *within us*: in our spirit, through it, as the memory of our own person.

Notes

1   For a more detailed treatment of these and other related questions which can only be touched upon here, see T. Georgiades, *Musik und Rhythmus bei den Griechen: zum Ursprung der abendländischen Musik* (Rowohlts deutsche Enzyklopädie 61), Hamburg 1958, 2nd ed. Kassel 1974 (Engl. transl. *Greek Music, Verse and Dance*, New York 1956). Concerning the relationship between music and language in antiquity, the transformation of ancient Greek and the contrast between this and modern Western languages – in particular between its concept of verse and that of the German language – see T. Georgiades, *Der griechische Rhythmus: Musik, Reigen, Vers und Sprache*, Hamburg 1949, 2nd ed. 1976.

2   J.A. Jungmann, *Missarum Sollemnia: eine genetische Erklärung der römischen Messe*, Vienna 1948, 5th ed. 1962 (Engl. transl. *The Mass of the Roman Rite: Its Origins and Development*, New York 1951, abridged ed. New York 1959, 2nd ed. 1961). I am indebted to this outstanding work on liturgical history

for an abundance of information – more in fact than I can
undertake to cite in detail in the following.

3   Ed. M. Gerbert in *Scriptores ecclesiastici de musica sacra* I,
St. Blasien 1784, repr. Hildesheim 1963, see 165ff. (A new
edition has been prepared by Hans Schmid: *Musica et Scolica
Enchiriadis*, Munich 1981.) See also E. Waeltner, *Die Lehre
vom Organum bis zur Mitte des 11. Jahrhunderts* (Münchner
Veröffentlichungen zur Musikgeschichte 13), Tutzing 1975.

4   The notational signs here employed have no rhythmic significance.

5   Concerning the Nordic preference for sonorities see R.v.
Ficker, "Primäre Klangformen," *Jahrbuch der Musikbibliothek
Peters* 36 (1929), 21ff. This pioneering study opens up new
pathways to the investigation of music history. On the
reinforcement of sonorities see further the same author's
preface to his edition of *Perotinus: Organum quadruplum
"Sederunt principes"*, Vienna 1930, and his article "Die Musik
des Mittelalters und ihre Beziehungen zum Geistesleben,"
*Deutsche Vierteljahrsschrift für Literaturwissenschaft und
Geistesgeschichte* 3 (1925), 501ff. The testimony of earlier
authors on the music of the Germanic peoples can be found in
H.J. Moser, *Geschichte der deutschen Musik* I (Stuttgart
1920), 5th ed. Stuttgart 1930, 34ff.

6   Ed. E. de Coussemaker in *Histoire de l'harmonie au moyen-
âge*, Paris 1852, repr. Hildesheim 1966, 229ff. New ed. by
H.H. Eggebrecht and F. Zaminer, *Ad organum faciendum*,
Mainz 1970, 43ff.

7   See Waeltner, *Die Lehre vom Organum bis zur Mitte des 11.
Jahrhunderts*.

8   See F. Zaminer, *Der Vatikanische Organum-Traktat (Ottob.
lat. 3025)* (Münchner Veröffentlichungen zur Musikgeschichte
2), Tutzing 1959. The significance of this treatise had previously been pointed out by R.v. Ficker, "Der Organumtraktat
der Vatikanischen Bibliothek Ottob. 3025," *Kirchen-
musikalisches Jahrbuch* 27 (1932), 65ff.

9   On this question see T. Georgiades, "Die musikalische
Interpretation," *Studium Generale* 7 (1954), 389ff, repr. in
Georgiades, *Kleine Schriften* (Münchner Veröffentlichungen
zur Musikgeschichte 26), Tutzing 1977, 45ff. See further
Georgiades, *Musik und Schrift*, Munich, 1962, 2nd ed.
1964.

10   On the thirteenth-century motet see F. Ludwig in Adler's
Handbuch der Musikgeschichte, Frankfurt am Main 1924,
198ff, 2nd ed. Berlin 1930 and repr. Munich 1975, 232ff;
further, see E.H. Sanders, "The Medieval Motet," *Gattungen
der Musik in Einzeldarstellungen. Gedenkschrift Leo Schrade*,
Bern 1973, 497ff.

11   Ed. E. de Coussemaker, Tournai 1861. Recent editions: L.
Schrade, *Polyphonic Music of the Fourteenth Century* I,

Monaco 1956, 110ff; C. van den Borren, *Missa Tornacensis* (*Corpus Mensurabilis Musicae* ser. 13), 1957.

12 Participants in the discussion on *fauxbourdon* include H. Besseler, M. Bukofzer, R.v. Ficker, T. Georgiades, and more recently H. Flasdieck and N.L. Wallin; their views diverge sharply in some respects. For more recent contributions see the studies by R.v. Ficker, H. Besseler, and H. Flasdieck in *Acta Musicologica* 23 (1951), 24 (1952), 25 (1953) and 29 (1957).

The above presentation is adapted from T. Georgiades, *Englische Diskanttraktate aus der 1. Hälfte des 15. Jahrhunderts: Untersuchungen zur Entwicklung der Mehrstimmigkeit im Mittelalter*, Munich 1937, from which Ex. 17 is taken.

For a summary of the various views concerning *fauxbourdon* and the most recent bibliography see Ann B. Scott, "The Beginnings of Fauxbourdon: A New Interpretation," *Journal of the American Musicological Society* 24 (1971), 345ff; further R. Bockholdt, "Englische und franko-flämische Kirchenmusik in der ersten Hälfte des 15. Jahrhunderts," *Geschichte der katholischen Kirchenmusik* I, ed. K.G. Fellerer, Kassel 1973, 427ff.

13 Taken from the edition in *Denkmäler der Tonkunst in Österreich* 31, 114. For a discussion of this work see R.v. Ficker, "Die frühen Messenkompositionen der Trienter Codices," *Studien zur Musikwissenschaft* 11, Vienna 1924, 52ff.

14 Ed. G. Malipiero in *Tutte le opere di Claudio Monteverdi* 14, Asolo 1932, 57ff.

15 The form *lebendig* constitutes a noteworthy exception, which can, however, be explained etymologically. Introduced as a more emphatic form of the adjective *lebend*, it was originally accented in the same way, that is on the first syllable. Accentuation of the second syllable, first introduced in some of the northern dialects, was not generally accepted until the eighteenth century. See F. Kluge, *Etymologisches Wörterbuch der deutschen Sprache* (Berlin 1883), 20th ed. 1967 rev. by W. Mitzka, 429.

16 See further T. Georgiades, *Schubert. Musik und Lyrik*, Göttingen 1967, 183ff.

17 Published in facsimile by J. Wolf, Kassel 1934.

18 Ed. G. Buchwald in *M. Joh. Mathesius, D. Martin Luthers Leben in 17 Predigten*, Leipzig 1887, 292.

19 *D. Martin Luthers Werke; Kritische Gesamtausgabe* XVIII, Weimar 1908, 123 ("Wider die himmlischen Propheten"); Engl. transl. from *Luther's Works, American Edition* XL, ed. Conrad Bergendorff (transl. by Bernhard Erling), Philadelphia 1958, 141.

20 K. Ameln et al., *Handbuch der deutschen evangelischen Kirchenmusik* I/1, Göttingen 1941, No. 349.

21 Ex. 30b (Johann Walther, 1530): ed. O. Kade, *Die ältere*

Passionskomposition bis zum Jahre 1631, Gütersloh 1893, repr. New York 1971.

22   Ed. P. Spitta in *Schütz-Gesamtausgabe* 12, Leipzig 1892, 117ff.

23   *Handbuch der deutschen evangelischen Kirchenmusik* I/1, No. 63; Walther's version is No. 65.

24   For a more detailed discussion of this point see Jungmann, *Missarum Sollemnia* I, Vienna 1948, 180–9, and 5th ed. 1962, 187–97 (for Engl. transl. see above, note 2).

25   Published (from F. Ludwig's papers) by H. Besseler in *Guillaume de Machaut: Musikalische Werke* 4, Leipzig 1943, 2nd ed. 1954. New ed. by L. Schrade, *Polyphonic Music of the Fourteenth Century* III, Monaco 1956, 37ff.

26   Ed. D. Plamenac in *Johannes Ockeghem: Collected Works* 2, New York 1947, 2nd corr. ed. 1966, 65ff.

27   From this point onward, for many of the examples discussed the reader is referred to any of the readily accessible editions of the works in question. Bach's chorale prelude *Vor deinen Thron* is given both in editions of the chorale preludes and as an appendix to *The Art of Fugue* (see for example the edition of the latter by W. Graeser, *Veröffentlichungen der Neuen Bach-Gesellschaft* 28/1, 119).

28   The above-quoted examples and their description are taken (the latter in part verbatim) from my two earlier articles "Aus der Musiksprache des Mozart-Theaters," *Mozart-Jahrbuch* 1950, 76ff, and "Zur Musiksprache der Wiener Klassiker," *Mozart-Jahrbuch* 1951, 50ff (both repr. in Georgiades, *Kleine Schriften*, 9ff and 33ff). The opera finales are discussed in the first of these articles (*Mozart-Jahrbuch* 50, 94ff and Tables I and II; *Kleine Schriften*, 26ff and the tables on 24f).

29   For the thorough analysis of Palestrina's polyphony we are indebted to the pioneering studies of Knud Jeppesen: *Der Palestrinastil und die Dissonanz*, Leipzig 1925 (Engl. transl. *The Style of Palestrina and the Dissonance*, London 1927, 3rd ed. New York 1970), and *Kontrapunkt; Lehrbuch der klassischen Vokalpolyphonie*, Leipzig 1935, 8th ed. Wiesbaden 1978 (Engl. transl. *Counterpoint: The Polyphonic Vocal Style of the Sixteenth Century*, New York 1939, 5th ed. 1960).

30   The continuous flow of Palestrina's music is reminiscent of prose. Even the instrumental polyphony of the thorough-bass era, however, in spite of its prominent metrical beat (see p. 76 above), still retains something of the attitude peculiar to prose. See also Georgiades, *Der griechische Rhythmus*, 41f.

31   See also the previous note. That remark, however, addressed itself to the rhythmic impression made by the flow of the music; here, on the other hand, the reference is to the content and its significance.

32   For the passages here discussed the reader is referred to the readily accessible Hawkes Pocket Scores editions of the work (Boosey & Hawkes, London).

33 For a more detailed discussion of this and of the following, see Georgiades, *Der griechische Rhythmus*, 141f and chapter 6 passim, and Georgiades, *Musik und Rhythmus bei den Griechen*, 45f and 59–63 (Engl. transl. *Greek Music, Verse and Dance*, 107ff and 143–53).